T0194771

An Analysis of

W. E. B. Du Bois's

The Souls of
Black Folk

Jason Xidias

Published by Macat International Ltd
24:13 Coda Centre, 189 Munster Road, London SW6 6AW.

Distributed exclusively by Routledge
2 Park Square, Milton Park, Abingdon, Oxon OX14 4RN
711 Third Avenue, New York, NY 10017, USA

Routledge is an imprint of the Taylor & Francis Group, an informa business

www.macat.com
info@macat.com

Cataloguing in Publication Data
A catalogue record for this book is available from the British Library.
Library of Congress Cataloguing-in-Publication Data is available upon request.
Cover illustration: Capucine Deslouis

ISBN 978-1-912303-71-7 (hardback)
ISBN 978-1-912127-56-6 (paperback)
ISBN 978-1-912282-59-3 (e-book)

Notice
The information in this book is designed to orientate readers of the work under analysis,
to elucidate and contextualise its key ideas and themes, and to aid in the development
of critical thinking skills. It is not meant to be used, nor should it be used, as a
substitute for original thinking or in place of original writing or research. References and
notes are provided for informational purposes and their presence does not constitute
endorsement of the information or opinions therein. This book is presented solely for
educational purposes. It is sold on the understanding that the publisher is not engaged
to provide any scholarly advice. The publisher has made every effort to ensure that
this book is accurate and up-to-date, but makes no warranties or representations with
regard to the completeness or reliability of the information it contains. The information
and the opinions provided herein are not guaranteed or warranted to produce particular
results and may not be suitable for students of every ability. The publisher shall not be
liable for any loss, damage or disruption arising from any errors or omissions, or from
the use of this book, including, but not limited to, special, incidental, consequential or
other damages caused, or alleged to have been caused, directly or indirectly, by the
information contained within.

CONTENTS

THE MACAT LIBRARY

The Macat Library is a series of unique academic explorations of seminal works in the humanities and social sciences – books and papers that have had a significant and widely recognised impact on their disciplines. It has been created to serve as much more than just a summary of what lies between the covers of a great book. It illuminates and explores the influences on, ideas of, and impact of that book. Our goal is to offer a learning resource that encourages critical thinking and fosters a better, deeper understanding of important ideas.

Each publication is divided into three Sections: Influences, Ideas, and Impact. Each Section has four Modules. These explore every important facet of the work, and the responses to it.

This Section-Module structure makes a Macat Library book easy to use, but it has another important feature. Because each Macat book is written to the same format, it is possible (and encouraged!) to cross-reference multiple Macat books along the same lines of inquiry or research. This allows the reader to open up interesting interdisciplinary pathways.

To further aid your reading, lists of glossary terms and people mentioned are included at the end of this book (these are indicated by an asterisk [*] throughout) – as well as a list of works cited.

Macat has worked with the University of Cambridge to identify the elements of critical thinking and understand the ways in which six different skills combine to enable effective thinking.
Three allow us to fully understand a problem; three more give us the tools to solve it. Together, these six skills make up the **PACIER** model of critical thinking. They are:

ANALYSIS – understanding how an argument is built
EVALUATION – exploring the strengths and weaknesses of an argument
INTERPRETATION – understanding issues of meaning

CREATIVE THINKING – coming up with new ideas and fresh connections
PROBLEM-SOLVING – producing strong solutions
REASONING – creating strong arguments

To find out more, visit **WWW.MACAT.COM.**

CRITICAL THINKING AND *THE SOULS OF BLACK FOLK*

Primary critical thinking skill: REASONING
Secondary critical thinking skill: CREATIVE THINKING

W.E.B Du Bois' *The Souls of Black Folk* is a seminal work in the field of sociology, a classic of American literature – and a solid example of carefully-structured reasoning.

One of the most important texts ever written on racism and black identity in America, the work contains powerful arguments that illustrate the problem of the position of black people in the US at the turn of the 20th-century. Du Bois identified three significant issues ('the color line'; 'double consciousness'; and 'the veil') that acted as roadblocks to true black emancipation, and showed how each of these in turn contributed to the problem of inequality.

Du Bois carefully investigates all three problems, constructing clear explanations of their significance in shaping the consciousness of a community that has been systematically discriminated against, and dealing brilliantly with counter-arguments throughout. *The Souls of Black Folk* went on to profoundly influence the civil rights movement in the US, inspiring post-colonial thinking worldwide.

ABOUT THE AUTHOR OF THE ORIGINAL WORK

W. E. B. Du Bois was born in 1868, part of a small, free, land-owning black population in Massachusetts. He was an excellent scholar and became the first African American to earn a PhD from Harvard University. Yet Du Bois had experienced racism first hand, especially when studying in the American South. That made him determined to promote equality throughout his life as a teacher, journalist, and political activist. Du Bois died at the grand age of 95 in the newly-independent Ghana.

ABOUT THE AUTHOR OF THE ANALYSIS

Dr Jason Xidias holds a PhD in European Politics from King's College London, where he completed a comparative dissertation on immigration and citizenship in Britain and France. He was also a Visiting Fellow in European Politics at the University of California, Berkeley. Currently, he is Lecturer in Political Science at New York University.

ABOUT MACAT

GREAT WORKS FOR CRITICAL THINKING

Macat is focused on making the ideas of the world's great thinkers accessible and comprehensible to everybody, everywhere, in ways that promote the development of enhanced critical thinking skills.

It works with leading academics from the world's top universities to produce new analyses that focus on the ideas and the impact of the most influential works ever written across a wide variety of academic disciplines. Each of the works that sit at the heart of its growing library is an enduring example of great thinking. But by setting them in context – and looking at the influences that shaped their authors, as well as the responses they provoked – Macat encourages readers to look at these classics and game-changers with fresh eyes. Readers learn to think, engage and challenge their ideas, rather than simply accepting them.

'Macat offers an amazing first-of-its-kind tool for interdisciplinary learning and research. Its focus on works that transformed their disciplines and its rigorous approach, drawing on the world's leading experts and educational institutions, opens up a world-class education to anyone.'

Andreas Schleicher
Director for Education and Skills, Organisation for Economic Co-operation and Development

'Macat is taking on some of the major challenges in university education ... They have drawn together a strong team of active academics who are producing teaching materials that are novel in the breadth of their approach.'

Prof Lord Broers,
former Vice-Chancellor of the University of Cambridge

'The Macat vision is exceptionally exciting. It focuses upon new modes of learning which analyse and explain seminal texts which have profoundly influenced world thinking and so social and economic development. It promotes the kind of critical thinking which is essential for any society and economy. This is the learning of the future.'

Rt Hon Charles Clarke, former UK Secretary of State for Education

'The Macat analyses provide immediate access to the critical conversation surrounding the books that have shaped their respective discipline, which will make them an invaluable resource to all of those, students and teachers, working in the field.'

Professor William Tronzo, University of California at San Diego

WAYS IN TO THE TEXT

KEY POINTS

- The teaching, research, journalism and activism of W. E. B. Du Bois (1868–1963) shaped the movements that ended racial segregation in the United States and colonialism in Africa and Asia.

- *The Souls of Black Folk* puts forward the idea that whites invented the concept of racism to advance their material wealth. This had serious negative consequences for black identity, democracy and humanity and could only be overcome by black pride, resistance and struggle.

- Souls went against the dominant view in early twentieth century America that blacks were biologically inferior to whites, which explained their position in society.

Who Was W. E. B. Du Bois?

William Edward Burghardt Du Bois was born in Great Barrington, Massachusetts in 1868. He excelled as a scholar and in 1895 became the first African American to earn a PhD from Harvard University. He went on to become a professor, journalist and activist, making huge contributions to society. Throughout his life he exposed the actual causes of racism in the United States and elsewhere, while explaining the effects racism had on black identity. He continually stressed the need to overcome racism to achieve genuine democracy and greater human understanding. Du Bois revived, then continued, the great legacy of Frederick Douglass,* who escaped slavery to become a prominent black intellectual. Du Bois became a central force in shaping the movements that ended racial segregation in the United States and colonialism in Africa and Asia and so can be considered one of history's great figures.

What Does *The Souls of Black Folk* Say?

W. E. B. Du Bois published *The Souls of Black Folk* in 1903. It consists of 14 essays on racism, some of which had already been published in the literary and cultural magazine, the *Atlantic Monthly.** These essays draw from the author's personal experiences and research.

In *Souls*, Du Bois uses a range of literary techniques to describe the conditions of racism and inequality in what was known as Jim Crow* America. This long period began in 1877 and ended in the 1960s. During this era, state governments implemented a variety of measures that encouraged racism, segregation and inequality. These measures were then reinforced by national Federal legislation. All of this took place despite the fact that the Thirteenth Amendment to the American Constitution* had abolished slavery in 1865 and the Fifteenth Amendment, passed in 1870, granted blacks the right to vote.

Souls challenged the dominant academic and mainstream position at the time that claimed blacks were both biologically and culturally inferior to whites. The British naturalist Charles Darwin* was one person who advanced this view. Du Bois opposed this claim in detail by showing how whites invented the concept of "racism" to advance their material wealth.

In *Souls* he argues that "the color line"—a metaphor he uses for racism—is and will be the greatest problem America faces in the twentieth century. In Du Bois's view, racism undermined both democracy and humanity. For America to truly be "one nation, indivisible under God," as the country so often claimed it was, whites would have to acknowledge the past and blacks would have to be equal citizens. Du Bois drew from German philosopher G. W. F. Hegel's* analysis of history and consciousness (or the awareness of oneself) in his 1807 book *The Phenomenology of Spirit* to argue that racism prevented both white and black Americans from fulfilling their potential.

Like Frederick Douglass before him, Du Bois encouraged blacks to become educated, to become leaders, to take pride in their heritage and culture and to struggle against white oppression. This position was in contrast to the view of Booker T. Washington,* another great African American figure of the time. Washington argued that blacks should accommodate white racism in exchange for a basic education and basic legal rights.

In *Souls*, Du Bois introduces two important concepts that further develop his idea of "the color line." The first is "double consciousness," which refers to the difficulties blacks face attempting to be both African and American in a white racist society. The second is "the veil," which metaphorically refers to racism as a kind of frontier dividing blacks and whites. This weighs heavily on both black and white souls and prevents both of them from achieving their full potential.

Throughout the text Du Bois makes it clear he is optimistic that one day America will lift this "veil." He believes this will happen when whites acknowledge the injustices of the past and blacks become equal citizens. When the veil is finally lifted, America will be a true democracy, humanity in general will transcend everything else and the American soul will be at peace.

Why Does *The Souls of Black Folk* Matter?

In *Souls*, Du Bois went against accepted early twentieth-century American thinking that blacks were biologically inferior to whites, presenting an alternative to Booker T. Washington's accommodationist stance. Du Bois achieved this by suggesting the capitalist* economic system led white people to be racist, and by encouraging black struggle. The text provides real insight into what shapes discrimination, how it conditions identity and how it must be overcome. Although Du Bois focused *The Souls of Black Folk* entirely on Jim Crow America, his later work addressed racism at a global level and was in favor of the collective struggle of all oppressed minorities. Du Bois's body of work—and *Souls* in particular—has inspired activists around the world. *Souls* lies at the intersection of African American studies, critical race and ethnicity theory and postcolonial studies. The book has huge interdisciplinary value, because it has been a starting point for further scholarship in a number of fields, ranging from history to sociology and from economics to politics.

SECTION 1
INFLUENCES

THE AUTHOR AND THE HISTORICAL CONTEXT

KEY POINTS

- *The Souls of Black Folk* is a seminal work in the field of sociology and a classic of American literature. It is one of the most important texts ever written on racism and black identity in America.

- Du Bois gained a much deeper understanding of racism in America in 1885 when he moved from Massachusetts in the north to study in Tennessee in the south.

- The Jim Crow* era was a period when state and local governments passed laws that discriminated against blacks. It started in 1877 and lasted until the civil rights movements of the 1960s.

Why Read This Text?

The Souls of Black Folk is a collection of 14 essays about racism written by American historian, sociologist and civil rights activist W. E. B. Du Bois. Published in 1903, it is one of the most important texts ever written in the field of sociology and is a classic of American literature. *Souls* is an essential read for anyone who wants to understand the many different elements that make up the history of black Americans. These include:

- Their identity and their awareness of it (consciousness)
- The discrimination and inequality they have experienced
- Links between racism and economics
- The role of education and leadership in shaping change
- The need to overcome injustice to reach a greater level of humanity

> ❝ History cannot ignore W. E. B. Du Bois because history has to reflect truth and Dr. Du Bois was a tireless explorer and a gifted discoverer of social truths. His singular greatness lay in his quest for truth about his own people. There were very few scholars who concerned themselves with honest study of the black man and he sought to fill this immense void. The degree to which he succeeded disclosed the great dimensions of the man. ❞
> Dr. Martin Luther King Jr.

Du Bois combines social analysis, religious references, literary metaphors and scientific research (using many different methods) in his work. All this leads to a mature, in-depth analysis of racism in late nineteenth and early twentieth century America and the struggle of blacks to overcome it. Throughout *Souls* the author puts across a sense of sorrow, but also one of deep optimism. Du Bois believed that one day black resistance and struggle would overcome the Jim Crow laws that legalized segregation at state and local levels and which led to black oppression and inequality. As he prophetically puts it in the text: "Someday the Awakening will come, when the pent-up vigor of ten-million souls shall sweep irresistibly towards the Goal, out of the Valley of the Shadow of Death."*[1]

Throughout the essays, Du Bois puts across a core message. Racism is a social construction that uses race, class and gender for political and economic ends. Its aim is to categorize, humiliate and exploit black people, primarily to make money. This, he says, can be seen in his current-day reality, as well as in the history of American slavery. The author argues that only a "Great Awakening" of black pride, resistance and struggle can overcome racism. In reality, this meant blacks having not only equal legal citizenship and the right to vote, but also the same opportunities as whites in education and employment. Only in these circumstances could everyone move on from past suffering and enjoy a greater sense of common humanity for whites and blacks alike.

Author's Life

William Edward Burghardt Du Bois was born in 1868 in Great Barrington, Massachusetts. Because his mother was a descendant not only of Africans but also of English and Dutch ancestors, William was part of a very small, free, land-owning black population. His mother, Mary, worked as a domestic servant and his father, Alfred, was unemployed, which meant that money was tight. Alfred abandoned the family only a year after William was born and never returned. Mary died when William was just 17, turning him into a poor orphan.

Du Bois attended a mostly white school and worshiped at a mainly white Protestant* church. Naturally intelligent, he became the first black graduate of his high school in 1884, earning high honors. With money he saved from working and with financial help from his local church, Du Bois enrolled at Fisk University in Nashville, Tennessee. There he earned a Bachelor of Arts degree, before adding another in History from Harvard University in his native Massachusetts. His experiences at Fisk in the American south, where the Jim Crow laws were fully embraced, shaped his views on society forever. It was there that Du Bois came to deeply understand racism in America and how it affected black identity.[2]

Du Bois never felt a part of Harvard but he understood how important studying at one of America's most respected universities was for his intellectual development and reputation. He always stressed that good education was the main way for blacks to become socially mobile and to challenge oppression. Du Bois became Harvard's first African American doctoral graduate. His Ph dissertation, written in the Department of History, was entitled "The Suppression of the African Slave-Trade to the United States of America, 1638–1870." At this time he also studied at Friedrich Wilhelm University in Berlin, investigating the work of sociologists and philosophers Max Weber,* Karl Marx* and other important German scholars.[3] Influenced by socialist ideas,[4] it was around this time that Du Bois first wrote of his desire to "work for the rise of the Negro people."[5] For the rest of his life he promoted equality through his academic scholarship and teaching (at Wilberforce University, the University of Pennsylvania, and Atlanta University), as well as through his journalism and political activism.

Author's Background

Du Bois published his most important work, *The Souls of Black Folk*, in 1903 against the backdrop of the Jim Crow laws. In 1870 the American Congress* passed the Fifteenth Amendment to the country's Constitution,* granting African Americans the right to vote. Yet from 1877 and the end of Reconstruction*—the rebuilding of the country following the Civil War* of 1861-65—right through to the civil rights movement of the 1960s, white southerners put an abundance of measures in place to stop blacks from achieving equality. For example, from 1890 to 1910 new state constitutions and laws imposed taxes and literacy tests that were deliberately designed to stop blacks from voting, even though they already had that right by law. Anyone who could not pay the taxes that were suddenly part of voting registration or could not read was not allowed to vote. White intimidation of blacks also hindered progress.

The 1896 Supreme Court case *Plessy versus Ferguson,** meanwhile, established that the federal government could not intervene to prevent states from imposing local segregation laws in many important areas, including employment, housing and public transportation.[6]

When Du Bois decided to leave Massachusetts in 1885 and attend Fisk University in Tennessee he understood that he would gain a much deeper understanding of racism in America. As he put it, "I was going into the South; the South of slavery, rebellion and black folk; above all, I was going to meet colored people of my own age and education, of my own ambition."[7]

At Fisk, Du Bois quickly noticed that white southerners were bitter over their defeat in the Civil War—where the southern states had failed to break away from the existing Union—and the abolition of slavery in 1865. Furthermore, he witnessed blacks suffering from extreme poverty, lack of opportunity and violence. As he put it, "No one but a Negro going into the South without previous experience of color caste can have any conception of its barbarism … I only sensed scorn and hate; the kind of despising which a dog might incur … Murder, killing and maiming Negroes, raping Negro women … this was not even news; it got no publicity, it caused no arrest."[8]

It was this historical backdrop of Jim Crow racism coupled with Du Bois's own experiences living in the American north and south—and Europe as well—that pushed him to become an intellectual leader of the Negro cause and of blacks everywhere. Du Bois's passion for justice lasted from the last decade of the nineteenth century until his death in newly-independent Ghana in 1963 at the grand age of 95.

NOTES

1 W. E. B. Du Bois, *The Souls of Black Folk* (New York and London: W.W. Norton and Company, 1999), xxxi.

2 Du Bois, *The Souls of Black Folk*, xiii–xv.

3 Du Bois, *The Souls of Black Folk*, xvi–xix.

4 Zhang Zuguo, *W. E. B. Du Bois: The Question for the Abolition of the Color Line* (New York: Routledge, 2001), 135.

5 Du Bois, *The Souls of Black Folk*, xvii, xviii.

6 J. Morgan Kousser, *The Shaping of Southern Politics: Suffrage, Restrictions and the Establishment of the One-Party South*, 1880-1910 (New Haven: Yale University Press, 1974).

7 Du Bois, *The Souls of Black Folk*, 1999, xxv.

8 Du Bois, *The Souls of Black Folk*, 1999, xxv.

ACADEMIC CONTEXT

KEY POINTS

- Du Bois argued that whites socially constructed—or invented the concept of—"race" to advance their own interests. This argument challenged the dominant view that blacks were biologically and culturally inferior to whites.
- Du Bois was inspired by the struggles of Frederick Douglass who escaped slavery and became a notable black intellectual leader in the nineteenth century.
- Du Bois adapted German philosopher G. W. F. Hegel's* understanding of the relationship between history and consciousness* to the study of racism in America and the divided consciousness of African Americans.

The Work In Its Context

Sociology—the scientific study of social behavior—is a relatively modern idea dating back to the late eighteenth century. The discipline developed as a response to advances in science, a decline in the influence of religion, industrialization and urbanization (the shift of population from rural to urban areas).

When W. E. B. Du Bois published *The Souls of Black Folk* in 1903 most sociologists believed that human progress occurred as our species evolved at a biological level. Herbert Spencer,* an early English sociologist of the mid-nineteenth century, was a champion of this view. His views were closely associated with those of the famous English naturalist* Charles Darwin,* who published *On the Origin of Species* (1859) and *The Descent of Man* (1871). Darwin argued that the "white and black races" differed from each other in intellectual capability.[1]

> **❝** The white man's happiness cannot be purchased by the black man's misery. Virtue cannot prevail among the white people, by its destruction among the black people... It is evident that white and black 'must fall or flourish together.' **❞**
>
> Frederick Douglass,* *Frederick Douglass: Selected Speechings and Writings*

These ideas developed out of the Enlightenment* movement of the late eighteenth century which looked to human reason and science for answers. In America, arguments in favor of evolutionary biology* like Spencer's highlighted the "stalled development" and "primitive nature" of black people. European colonial powers were quick to justify their expansion into Africa and Asia and their exploitation of these countries by spreading the idea that they were naturally superior to the native people who lived there. They claimed that, in fact, it was their *duty* to guide these people towards a "higher state of being." This idea is sometimes referred to as "the White Man's Burden"[2] after a poem of the same name by the Englishman Rudyard Kipling.* This expansion into other territories was also called the civilizing mission.*

Rapid industrialization and urbanization took place in America after the Civil War* as huge numbers of people—many of them black—flocked to cities in search of work. Academics started to use the scientific method* to study social conditions in the United States. This approach involves posing a question and predicting what the answer may be, then carrying out tests and experiments to prove whether that answer is true or false. Several universities began offering PhD programs in sociology and in 1895 W. E. B. Du Bois became the first African American to receive a doctorate from Harvard.

The Souls of Black Folk made a groundbreaking contribution to the field of sociology by challenging the dominant set of beliefs that white people were racially superior. The book argued that white elites in the United States deliberately created a society in which racism was rife and that inequality was a direct result of capitalism* and the country's history of black slavery. These two factors made it extremely difficult for black people to progress.

Overview of the Field

French philosopher Auguste Comte* is widely regarded as a founding father of sociology[3] and his work *A General View of Positivism* (1848) first introduced the idea of using the scientific method of the natural sciences to study the structure of society.

Inspired by rational, science-based Enlightenment thought, he argued that social evolution consisted of three phases. The first was theological, asserting that religion determined one's position in society. In other words, everyone had a "God-given" place on the social ladder. The King, for example, was at the top of the ladder because of his alleged unique relationship with God.

The second phase was metaphysical, a period during which rational scientific thought challenged the "God-given" phase by promoting a respect for universal rights and human progress. The French Revolution of 1789 and *The Declaration of the Rights of Man and of the Citizen** are examples of this.

The final phase was positivist, which meant actively applying the scientific method to the study of problems such as inequality, rather than merely accepting philosophies of natural rights and equalities put forward in works such as *The Declaration of the Rights of Man*.

Like Comte, German revolutionary socialist Karl Marx* applied the scientific method to understanding social change and progress. From the 1840s onwards he argued that history was a product of the struggle between the ruling class and the working class. He believed that workers would eventually unite to overthrow both the ruling class and capitalism itself and replace it with a communist* society free of exploitation. There are obvious parallels between Marx's view and Du Bois's argument that racism in the United States was based on economics, though it is worth noting that, at the time Du Bois was writing *Souls*, Marx's influence in American academia was limited.[4]

Academic Influences

American writer Ralph Waldo Emerson* coined the term "double consciousness" in his book *The Transcendentalist*, written in 1843. Du Bois extended this idea by applying the term to the social psychology of "race relations." He used it to explain the psychological state of having both an African heritage and either a European or American "upbringing" under slavery. Du Bois described this double consciousness as seeing your own life through other people's eyes.

At Harvard, Du Bois studied German philosophy and, in writing *Souls*, he drew on G. W. F. Hegel's *The Phenomenology of Spirit*. Professor of Literature Shamoon Zamir* has argued that Hegel gave Du Bois the means to theorize "the relationship of consciousness to history."[5]

In *Phenomenology*, Hegel used the example of the master and the slave to show how unequal power relations lead to a lack of recognition of the individual. This in turn obstructs a person's self-consciousness, or their knowledge of themselves as a person. It is necessary to be recognized as an autonomous (self-governing) individual by others in order to be free and self-realized (able to fulfill one's own potential). If there is no such recognition, the master defines the slave's identity and the slave's consciousness of himself as an individual is damaged, which results in the slave existing in an oppressed state.

Du Bois applies Hegel's concept to "post-emancipation America" (the period after slavery was abolished), arguing that white racism had serious consequences for black identity. African Americans had made significant gains during the period of Reconstruction following the end of the Civil War in 1865. These included the abolition of slavery, the prohibition of racial discrimination and the granting of citizenship and the right to vote. Despite this, Du Bois shows how the same power relations that existed under slavery had been reproduced by Jim Crow* laws which helped create discrimination in what was called a "separate but equal" society. This led as a result to a form of re-enslavement, with states prohibiting inter-ethnic marriages, imposing segregation between races and creating literacy tests* and poll taxes* specifically to prevent blacks from voting.

This re-enslavement, Du Bois argued, created a divided consciousness inside the mind of African Americans that could only be overcome by social conflict and an eventual white recognition of equality.

Finally, the work of Scottish philosopher Thomas Carlyle* influenced Du Bois's desire to be a leader of the black cause.[6] Carlyle advanced the Great Man Theory,* which argued that great men used their intelligence, wisdom, charisma and political acumen to make history. In this sense Du Bois hoped to succeed Frederick Douglass, the escaped slave who had become a black leader through scholarship, in guiding black resistance and struggle.

NOTES

1   Charles Darwin, *The Descent of Man* (London: John Murray, 1871), 216–7.

2   Rudyard Kipling, "The White Man's Burden," *McClure's Magazine* 12 (1899): 290–1.

3   See, for example, the back cover of: Auguste Comte, *Comte: Early Political Writings,* ed. H.S. Jones (Cambridge: Cambridge University Press, 1998).

4   There is a long-standing debate why the United States has never had a socialist influence/labor movement comparable to some European countries. This dates back to Alexis de Tocqueville's idea of "American exceptionalism." See, for example: Seymour Martin Lipset and Gary Marks, *It Didn't Happen Here: Why Socialism Failed in America* (New York: W.W. Norton & Company, 2001).

5   Shamoon Zamir, *W. E. B. Du Bois and American Thought*: *1888–1903* (Chicago: University of Chicago, 1995), 117.

6   For further details, see: Zhang Zuguo, *W. E. B. Du Bois: The Question for the Abolition of the Color Line* (New York: Routledge, 2001), *W. E. B.* 29.

THE PROBLEM

KEY POINTS

- The key question among black intellectuals at the time of publication of *The Souls of Black Folk* was: how can African Americans best advance their position in racist America?

- In 1895 Booker T. Washington,* a prominent black intellectual of the era, agreed with white southerners that blacks would accept white political rule in exchange for a basic education and basic legal rights, a settlement known as the Atlanta Compromise.*

- Du Bois argued that blacks should not make compromises and should struggle against white racism to achieve equality.

Core Question

The Souls of Black Folk addresses three core questions:

- Why do whites continue to oppress African Americans even after the Civil War* and Reconstruction*?
- How does racism affect African American identity?
- How can African Americans climb the social ladder in a racist society?

W. E .B. Du Bois responds to these questions with a combination of sorrow, suffering and hope.

For Du Bois, Frederick Douglass* had been "the greatest of American Negro leaders."[1] Douglass escaped from slavery and became a social reformer, public speaker and influential writer. He led the abolitionist movement* to end slavery and played a key role in shaping

> ❝ There can be no doubt of Mr. Washington's mistakes and shortcomings: he never adequately grasped the growing bond of politics and industry … In stern justice, we must lay on the soul of this man, a heavy responsibility for the consummation of Negro disenfranchisement, the decline of the Negro college and public school and the firmer establishment of color caste in this land. ❞
>
> W. E. B. Du Bois, *The Souls of Black Folk*

President Abraham Lincoln's* Emancipation Proclamation* of 1863, which stated that all slaves in the rebellious southern states would be free. During the course of his lifetime Douglass wrote three autobiographies in which he described profound racism in America and called for black struggle.

Du Bois was deeply affected by Douglass's death, so much so that he expressed his innermost feelings in a series of elegies* entitled *The Passing of Douglass*. Du Bois tried to revive and continue his legacy by becoming the new intellectual leader of the African American cause. He successfully continued Douglass's work by defending the view that racism was a white political–economic tool to exploit black labor.

The Participants

In 1845, Frederick Douglass published his first autobiography, *The Narrative of the Life of Frederick Douglass*. The text traces the life of the author and his escape from slavery, focusing on the masters' brutal domination of slaves and his own experience of being worked to complete exhaustion and whipped when he could work no longer. The text played an important role in the abolitionist movement of the mid-nineteenth century in the United States. It sold thousands of copies[2] when it was published and challenged the dominant white view that blacks were unintelligent and incapable of producing intellectual work. Douglass went on to publish two more autobiographies, *My Bondage and My Freedom* (1855) and *The Life and Times of Frederick Douglass* (1881).

Du Bois believed that Douglass had been the greatest of role models for blacks and was concerned that, after his death, Booker T. Washington had become the dominant figure in the African American community. Du Bois did not believe Washington represented the community's interests. In 1895, Washington criticized blacks for seeking political and economic power during Reconstruction and struck an agreement with white southerners called the Atlanta Compromise, which declared that southern blacks would submit to white political rule in exchange for a basic education and basic legal rights.

The Contemporary Debate

Washington argued that blacks should get over the injustices of the past, accept discrimination, undertake industrial education intended to get them into jobs, integrate into the dominant society and prove to whites through hard work and by being good consumers that they were worthy of better treatment. Under the Atlanta Compromise, blacks would not rise up against racism and would not demand the right to vote.

Du Bois strongly disagreed with Washington's stance, claiming that blacks would only perpetuate white oppression if they accepted this relationship. Du Bois's alternative proposed that blacks should resist all domination and wage a struggle for civic equality, the right to vote, equal education and the establishment of a true meritocracy in which individuals would be judged on their abilities, not on their race.

The Souls of Black Folk gave voice to a developing black collective consciousness (a sense of themselves as a group) and a shared black culture. This came at a time when former slaves and the children of slaves were struggling to gain a sense of who they were and what their community represented in the aftermath of the Civil War and Reconstruction. Du Bois was the leader of their resistance to white rule and the struggle born from the chaos of slavery. He also galvanized opposition to the Jim Crow laws at a time when clear attempts were being made to make African Americans officially inferior in civil terms, through segregation and by withdrawing aid from black educational institutions.

For these reasons, *Souls* was a highly significant response to the dominant position of whites and to the stance of Booker T. Washington, who was willing to work within the system to improve things for blacks. It provided an alternative view of racism in America and addressed how blacks should respond to it. But it also set out intellectual arguments for the way to achieve black progress and develop a black middle class.

NOTES

1   Du Bois, *The Souls of Black Folk*, xii.

2   Frederick Douglass, introduction to *Narrative of the Life of Frederick Douglass: an American Slave*, ed. Benjamin Quarles (Cambridge, MA: Harvard University Press, 1988).

THE AUTHOR'S CONTRIBUTION

KEY POINTS

- The ideas contained in *The Souls of Black Folk* revive the beliefs of former slave and black intellectual Frederick Douglass* and serve as an inspiration for blacks in America and elsewhere. They oppose the accommodationist stance of Booker T. Washington.*

- The book challenges the dominant view in academia and politics that blacks were biologically and culturally inferior to whites.

- Du Bois argues that racism in his country is an invented concept rooted in capitalism* and America's legacy of slavery. He believes that black resistance, pride, and struggle will eventually overcome prejudice.

Author's Aims

W. E. B. Du Bois's *The Souls of Black Folk* revived the legacy of former slave Frederick Douglass and put it back on the political agenda. Douglass had led the movement to abolish slavery in the United States and gained fame among blacks as a charismatic and persuasive writer and public speaker. He fought for universal equality, challenging the dominant white view that blacks were not intelligent enough to be intellectuals. His autobiographies depicted the horrors of slavery, but his escape and rise to prominence proved an inspiration to many.

After Douglass's death in 1895, Booker T. Washington became one of the most recognized black intellectuals in America. His view was that blacks should in the short term submit to racism and white political rule in exchange for basic concessions. By means of

> " Dr. Du Bois was not only an intellectual giant exploring the frontiers of knowledge, he was in the first place a teacher … One idea he insistently taught was that black people have been kept in oppression and deprivation by a poisonous fog of lies that depicted them as inferior, born deficient and deservedly doomed to servitude to the grave … The twisted logic ran if the black man was inferior he was not oppressed—his place in society was appropriate to his meager talent and intellect. "
>
> Dr. Martin Luther King Jr.

scholarship, journalism and activism, Du Bois challenged the view that blacks were biologically inferior to whites by showing how white capitalist greed depended on slavery and racism to make money from cheap labor. This position was revolutionary at the time and met with mixed reactions.[1]   Unlike Washington, who believed that blacks should accept being "second-class citizens," Du Bois argued that whites and blacks could overcome the injustice of the past and create a humane society grounded in equality.

Approach

In line with developments in sociology and the social sciences, Du Bois applied the scientific method* (working out answers to problems through experiments and the use of hard data) to understanding social problems—in this case racism and inequality—and their effects on African American identity.

Published in 1903, *The Souls of Black Folk* built on another seminal work by Du Bois, *The Philadelphia Negro*, which had appeared four years earlier. One of the earliest examples of sociology as a statistical science, the book combines more than 5,000 interviews with ordinary people together with census data[2] to present a vivid picture of the social and economic deprivation of African Americans living in Philadelphia, Pennsylvania.

Souls opened eyes because it confronted "the scientifically proven" position that inferior biological characteristics made black people incapable of achieving equality. Du Bois explained how whites had built a society in which they were seen as intellectually and morally superior by using the concept of "race differences" to exploit blacks in order to make money for themselves. He argued that, as a result, whites were imprisoned in their own self-denial. Du Bois explained this set-up more clearly in his later work *Black Construction*: "Out of the exploitation of the dark proletariat [black workers] comes the Surplus Value [profit] filched from human beasts ...The emancipation of man is the emancipation of labor and the emancipation of labor is the freeing of that basic majority of workers who are yellow, brown and black."[3]

Contribution In Context

Du Bois's analysis of racism in America built on the legacy of the abolitionist movement,* which was led by former slaves such as Frederick Douglass. Du Bois's renewed call for social struggle was a continuation of this earlier ideology but his approach was more scientific, incorporating the latest developments in the social sciences to make the link between economics and racism and inequality.

Although Du Bois drew from previous scholarship by the German philosopher G. W. F. Hegel,* among others, he addressed African American identity in a new way. He applied Hegel's link between history and consciousness—as well as psychological research on split personalities—to the condition of blacks in America. He showed how their identity issues and their inability to climb the social ladder was caused by white racism insisting that social conflict, rather than accommodation (or simply accepting racist behavior), was the best approach to overcoming oppression and inequality. By stressing education, pride and leadership, Du Bois also encouraged blacks to help American society become more humane.

It is tempting to draw parallels between Du Bois's interpretation of black exploitation based on white financial gain in America and the views of German philosopher Karl Marx.* Marx took the view that history is marked by the struggle between the workers and the ruling class. However, Du Bois made it clear that at this point in his academic career he had only a rudimentary understanding of Marxism.* As he put it, "[In my early work] there are some approaches, some allusions, but no complete realization of the application of the philosophy of Karl Marx to my subject. That concept came much later, when I began intensive study of the facts of society, culminating in my *Black Reconstruction* [1935]."[4]

NOTES

1   See: W. E. B. Du Bois, *The Souls of Black Folk* (New York and London: W.W. Norton and Company, 1999), 221–346.

2   See, for example, Greg Johnson, "W. E. B. Du Bois' The Philadelphia Negro," *Penn Current*, July 2, 2009, accessed January 20, 2015, http://www.upenn.edu/pennnews/current/node/3997.

3   W. E. B. Du Bois, *Black Reconstruction in America* (New York: Russell and Russell, 1963), 16.

4   W. E. B. Du Bois, *The Suppression of the African Slave Trade in the United States of America, 1638–1870* (New York: The Social Science Press, 1954), 327–9.

SECTION 2
IDEAS

MODULE 5
MAIN IDEAS

KEY POINTS

- Du Bois presents three core concepts in *Souls*: "the color line" (racism)—the main problem which confronts America in the twentieth century; "double consciousness"—the psychological challenge facing blacks as they attempt to be both African and American in a racist society; "the veil"—a metaphor referring to the barrier that racism creates between whites and blacks.

- The author's hope is that one day American society will transcend its racism, that democracy will be achieved and that all of humanity will be united.

- Du Bois feels both sorrow and pain at the racism he experiences and witnesses, but is still optimistic that a more just society will emerge.

Key Themes

In the foreword ("The Forethought") of *The Souls of Black Folk*, W. E. B. Du Bois states: "Herein lie buried many things which if read with patience may show the strange meaning of being black here in the dawning of the Twentieth Century. This meaning is not without interest to you, Gentle Reader; for the problem of the Twentieth Century is the problem of the color line."[1]

This description depicts racism as *the problem* in American society, and one that has long affected black and white people alike. This is the key theme that underpins the entire book. Du Bois then reflects on how this affects the way African Americans think about the society they live in and asks the question: "How does it feel to be a problem?"[2]

The author then answers: "To be a poor man is hard, but to be a

> ❝ The Nation has not yet found peace from its sins; the freedman has not yet found in freedom his promised land. Whatever of good may have come in these years of change, the shadow of a deep disappointment rests upon the Negro people. ❞
>
> W. E. B. Du Bois, *The Souls of Black Folk*

poor race in a land of dollars is the very bottom of hardships."[3]

Du Bois then discusses the legacy of the Civil War,* the Emancipation Proclamation,* the period of Reconstruction* and segregation and inequality implemented by the Jim Crow* laws. At this point he stresses the strong link between racism and capitalism.

Du Bois describes how slavery and the Jim Crow laws create a deeply engrained condition in the minds of African Americans. It is at this point that he introduces the two most important concepts of the text: double consciousness and the metaphor of the veil.

The author is also optimistic about the struggle against oppression. He emphasizes the importance of black leadership and—in contrast to another prominent black political figure, Booker T. Washington*— he argues that African Americans must engage in a social struggle which he hopes will one day bring about civic equality, the right to vote, equal education and the establishment of a meritocracy in which people are judged on their abilities alone.

Exploring The Ideas

The term "double consciousness" describes the fractured mental state of African Americans. This state is created by the daily challenge blacks face as they attempt to assimilate into a dominant white culture, while simultaneously trying to maintain a sense of pride in their own black heritage and identity. Du Bois depicts this condition as follows: "One ever feels his two-ness, an American, a Negro; two souls, two thoughts, two unreconciled strivings: two warring ideals in one dark body, whose dogged strength alone keeps it from being torn asunder."[4]

Du Bois then introduces his metaphor of "the veil," which represents the division between two worlds: a dominant white one and a politically, economically, and socially marginalized black one. The African American is constantly prevented from fulfilling his or her potential by a white, racist outlook that not only distorts reality but causes psychological torment to the black individual. As Du Bois puts it: "The Negro is … born with a veil, and gifted with second-sight in this American world, a world which yields him no true self-consciousness, but only lets him see himself through the revelation of the other world … This double-consciousness, this sense of always looking at one's self through the eyes of others, of measuring one's soul by the tape of a world that looks on in amused contempt and pity."[5]

In addressing this double consciousness, Du Bois talks about his own experience as a black man in this white world, describing how he was "… shut out from their world by a vast veil."[6] He illustrates his point with a story from his time at Fisk University when he gave a greeting card to a white girl who refused it on the grounds that he was a black man.

Du Bois describes three different ways that blacks react to this condition of double consciousness. They glorify their blackness to feel pride in themselves (the "Black is Beautiful"* movement of the 1960s is a good example). They seek revenge by revolting against the dominant society (as in the Black Power* movement, also in the 1960s). Or they try to adapt their behavior to white culture by assimilating into it.

Du Bois's hope is that through black pride, education, leadership and struggle blacks will transcend the veil and overcome the traumatic condition of double consciousness.

Language And Expression

Du Bois uses a variety of literary techniques, including metaphor, autobiography, Negro spirituals, biblical allusions and Greek mythology to persuade two distinct audiences of his case. The first of these is the dominant white society that stands on the other side of the veil and uses racism to marginalize African Americans. He talks about the injustices blacks suffer and calls for whites to reflect and show greater humanity. The second audience is the black society that stands behind the veil, is oppressed by the Jim Crow laws and seeks liberation from white domination. In a world of racism and inequality Du Bois hopes to lead and inspire the black reader by using a prophetic voice that highlights the rich history of African American culture, spirituality and struggle.

In addition to this range of literary techniques, Du Bois applies the scientific method* to his argument by linking sociology to economics. In particular, he emphasizes the relationship between white greed in a capitalist society and the racism and inequality suffered by the blacks who do the work.

The concepts of the "color line," "double consciousness," and "the veil" remain important to this day in the field of sociology and beyond.

NOTES

1 Du Bois, *The Souls of Black Folk*, 5.

2 Du Bois, *The Souls of Black Folk*, 9.

3 Du Bois, *The Souls of Black Folk*, 14.

4 Du Bois, *The Souls of Black Folk*, 11.

5 Du Bois, *The Souls of Black Folk*, 10–11.

6 Du Bois, *The Souls of Black Folk*, 10.

MODULE 6
SECONDARY IDEAS

KEY POINTS

- Du Bois addresses two secondary themes in the text. First, progress towards greater equality during the Reconstruction* period has been undermined by white bitterness over both the Civil War* and the abolition of slavery. Second, religion and the black church were great sources of inspiration for black pride, resistance, and struggle during the period of the Jim Crow* laws.

- Efforts to help freed slaves to integrate into white society such as the Freedmen's Bureau* were often undermined by resentful white people.

- Religion and the black Church provided refuge for blacks in a society that oppressed them and served as a source of inspiration for collective resistance to racism.

Other Ideas

W. E. B. Du Bois's *The Souls of Black Folk* is a collection of 14 essays written over seven years, so it naturally addresses a number of secondary themes. Two of the most important are contained in "On the Dawn of Freedom" and "Of the Faith of Our Fathers."

In "On the Dawn of Freedom" Du Bois explores the Freedmen's Bureau, a federal government agency that helped freed slaves integrate into white society during the era of Reconstruction between 1865 and 1877. It was set up by President Abraham Lincoln* in 1865 and provided educational services, legal help and employment to help blacks integrate. However, its efforts were largely undermined by white southerners (such as the violent supremacist group the Ku Klux Klan*) who were bitter over the loss of the Civil War and the abolition

> **❝** To be a poor man is hard, but to be a poor race in a land of dollars is the very bottom of hardships. **❞**
>
> W. E. B. Du Bois, *The Souls of Black Folk*

of slavery. The establishment of the Black Codes*—laws passed by southern states in 1865 and 1866 to continue white supremacy—also hindered the Bureau. Under these codes, the presence of any amount of black blood in a person's lineage made them legally black. Public facilities were segregated meaning, for example, that a black person could not use a bathroom intended for white people. Freedmen were obliged to work but they could not be taught to read and write and were not allowed to assemble without a white person being present. These codes were designed to make sure whites had a steady supply of cheap labor. They included vagrancy statutes, which permitted whites to arrest anyone they suspected of leaving their workplace; any black person who could not pay a fine would be sentenced to forced labor. In 1872, Ulysses Grant* became president and abruptly closed the Freedmen's Bureau because of southern opposition to help being given to blacks hoping to get on in life.

The essay "Of the Faith of our Fathers" describes the history and influence of the black Church in America and how religion had shaped, and was still shaping, African American culture and resistance. Du Bois focuses in particular on the important role black preachers, either former slaves or children of slaves, played in promoting solidarity in the black community.

Exploring The Ideas

In his essay "On the Dawn of Freedom," Du Bois makes one main argument: that despite claims that the Civil War began over issues of how much power each individual state should have compared to the Union, this was not the underlying cause of the war. For Du Bois, the real issue was that of slavery. "We knew that the question of Negro Slavery was the real cause of the conflict,"[1] he says.

In analyzing Reconstruction Du Bois argues that, although the Freedmen's Bureau was an important initiative, it was often undermined. While it helped freed slaves receive an education, granting them access to newly-established black schools like Fisk University, corrupt officials would often find ways to strip successful blacks of their property. As he explains, "in a distracted land where slavery had hardly fallen, to keep the strong from wanton abuse of the weak, and the weak from gloating insolently over the half-shorn strength of the strong, was a thankless, hopeless task."[2] Du Bois argues that, despite the abolition of slavery, the Jim Crow laws and other forms of racism in effect led to the re-enslavement of blacks.

In "Of the Faith of Our Fathers," Du Bois highlights the importance of religion as a uniting force among African Americans. He emphasizes the role preachers play in providing leadership in the struggle to overcome "the color line," using black faith and solidarity to transcend "the veil" and move towards liberty and justice.

Overlooked

Du Bois's work has had an enduring impact on race and ethnicity studies, as well as on post-colonial scholarship, which analyzes the material and cultural legacies of European colonialism. However, as scholars like Professor Robert Wortham* and Professor Earl Wright* have pointed out, sociologists often overlook Du Bois's influence.[3] His use of the scientific method* in the study of the condition of blacks in a political-economic context was ahead of its time, while his view of American society flew in the face of contemporary opinion which held that the position of blacks was due to "their inferior biological characteristics." These contributions put Du Bois among the most prominent sociologists of all time.

Post-colonial scholars such as Paul Gilroy* and Homi K. Bhabha* have brought back to the fore the subject of how the unequal relationship between blacks and whites conditioned identity. Gilroy has showcased how Du Bois's message linked the experiences of blacks, not just in America, but globally. As Du Bois said himself: "Peoples of the World, we American Negroes appeal to you; our treatment in America is not merely an internal question of the United States. It is a basic problem of humanity; of democracy; of discrimination because of race and color; and as such it demands your attention and action. No nation is so great that the world can afford to let it continue to be deliberately unjust, cruel, and unfair towards its own citizens."[4]

NOTES

1   Du Bois, *The Souls of Black Folk*, 17.

2   Du Bois, *The Souls of Black Folk*, 29–30.

3   Robert A. Wortham, "Introduction to the Sociology of W. E. B. Du Bois," *Sociation Today* 3 (2005): 1; Earl Wright, "W. E. B. Du Bois and the Atlanta Sociological Laboratory," *Sociation Today* 3 (2005): 1.

4   Excerpt from W. E. B. Du Bois, *An Appeal to the World: A Statement of Denial of Human Rights to Minorities in the Case of citizens of Negro Descent in the United States of America and an Appeal to the United Nations for Redress* (New York: National Association for the Advancement of Colored People, 1947).

MODULE 7
ACHIEVEMENT

KEY POINTS

- W. E. B. Du Bois challenged the dominant view in American society that racism existed because blacks were biologically inferior. He did this by showing how capitalism* used the idea of supposed black racial inferiority to justify cheap labor. This view inspired black struggles across the world.

- Du Bois did not agree with the more militant stance of Marcus Garvey,* who called on black Americans to abandon their country and return to their ancestral homeland.

- Du Bois saw huge advances in the black struggle during his lifetime, but his hope for human harmony has not been fully realized because racism still exists.

Assessing The Argument

As an academic researcher, teacher, journalist and activist, W. E. B. Du Bois encouraged black struggle on a global scale by highlighting the connection between capitalist greed and racism in the United States and beyond. He encouraged blacks to fight for equality and not to accept white political rule and discrimination in exchange for a few basic concessions. The three most important concepts in *The Souls of Black Folk*—the color line, double consciousness and the veil—continue to have an important influence on race and ethnicity studies and post-colonial studies.

Despite widespread racism in American society in 1903, *Souls* made an immediate impact. Only two months after publication it was in its third printing. Although the author had already published two books and numerous scholarly and journalistic articles, this was the

> 66 He [Du Bois] symbolized in his being his pride in the black man. He did not apologize for being black and, because of it, handicapped. Instead he attacked the oppressor for the crime of stunting black men. He confronted the establishment as a model of militant manhood and integrity. He defied them and, though they heaped venom and scorn on him, his powerful voice was never stilled. 99
>
> Dr. Martin Luther King Jr.

text that brought him international recognition. Important figures such as writer and literary critic Henry James* praised the book for its literary and social value. At the same time, many prominent southerners including another black leader, Booker T. Washington,* criticized Du Bois for stirring up "unnecessary" controversy.[1] Between 1903 and 1940 the text sold in the region of 20,000 copies. In 1953 the Blue Heron Press of New York published 1,000 copies of a 50-year commemoration edition, for which Du Bois supplied a new foreword. In 2003 commemoration events took place throughout the United States and elsewhere in appreciation of the author's legacy.[2] Despite all this, Du Bois's full intent has not been realized because racism and inequality still exist.

Achievement In Context

Building on the scholarship and activism of former slave Frederick Douglass,* Du Bois challenged white supremacy and Booker T. Washington's position that blacks should accept discrimination in exchange for modest advances in society. Yet he also opposed the more militant stance of Marcus Garvey.

Garvey was a Jamaican-born black nationalist* who founded the

Universal Negro Improvement Association* in 1914. He subsequently moved to Harlem, New York, where he argued for black purity and separation from white society, calling on all black Americans to "return" to their ancestral homeland, Africa. Although Du Bois commended Garvey for promoting black pride and confidence, he strongly disagreed with his views. Du Bois maintained that blacks were both African and American, and that neither aspect should at any point be lost. He believed that blacks could achieve equality in American society, while preserving the richness of their heritage and cultural identity, if they were properly led by an intellectual elite, or as he called it a "Talented Tenth."* Du Bois used the term to describe his original idea that one in 10 black men could become leaders and help their black fellow-men rise up. Du Bois thought that the process of black struggle and white recognition of black identity was required to cleanse the soul of both the oppressor and the oppressed, and to reach a higher state of humanity.

Souls has served as a foundation for a better understanding of racism and black identity and has provided inspiration for future black leaders and for liberation struggles, both in the United States and in former European colonies.

Although *Souls* argued for equal civil and political rights for blacks, as well as equal education and the establishment of a meritocracy, its aims have not been entirely fulfilled since publication in 1903. The author should, nevertheless, be remembered as one of the foremost sociologists in history and as someone who played an instrumental role in advancing the position of all the oppressed peoples of the world.

Limitations

The Souls of Black Folk applies first and foremost to racism and identity in the United States in the late nineteenth and early twentieth centuries. The text depicts a society that functions on white privilege and a dominant belief in white racial supremacy. As a result, blacks are second-class citizens.The 14 essays Du Bois wrote dealt with the Civil War,* slavery, Reconstruction,* the link between capitalism* and racism, the effects of racism on African American identity, religion and the black Church, pride, resistance, and struggle. The text also has a broader relevance, highlighting the ways in which whites in a capitalist society oppress ethnic minorities and how this holds back the whole of society, preventing democracy from functioning. *Souls* should be regarded as an interdisciplinary masterpiece relevant to more than one academic area of study and a text that has had considerable relevance over time.

NOTES

1   W. E. B. Du Bois, *The Souls of Black Folk* (New York and London: W.W. Norton and Company, 1999), 221–346.

2   University of Massachusetts Libraries, Special Collections, University Archives, DuBoisopedia, December 18, 2013, accessed January 20, 2015, http://scua.library.umass.edu/duboisopedia/doku.php?id= about:souls_of_black_folk.

PLACE IN THE AUTHOR'S WORK

KEY POINTS

- W. E. B. Du Bois's body of work was all about exposing racism and highlighting its effects on identity, consciousness, democracy and humanity, then encouraging a collective struggle to overcome it.

- *The Souls of Black Folk* was one of many significant elements in Du Bois's lifelong commitment to achieving greater human understanding.

- *Souls* built on a previous work, *The Philadelphia Negro,* and gave Du Bois international recognition. His struggle against oppression then took on a global perspective.

Positioning

In 1896 W. E. B. Du Bois was hired by the University of Pennsylvania, where he began studying the living conditions of blacks in Philadelphia. This research was very advanced for its time, incorporating several different methods including interviews, participant observation and historical and data analysis. As Du Bois's biographer Professor David Levering Lewis explains, "As he tabulated some 15,000 household schedules, he had before him life histories of the entire black population of the Seventh Ward, nearly 10,000 men, women, and children."[1]

This intensive research culminated in Du Bois's first seminal work, *The Philadelphia Negro*, which he published while working at Atlanta University in 1899. In 1903 Du Bois went on to publish *The Souls of Black Folk*, which again employed mixed research methods and further highlighted the conditions of racism and inequality in America. This

> ❝ Du Bois ... informed the reader that racism and discrimination not only stymied Blacks, but had serious repercussions for Whites whose fear, doubt, distrust, contempt, and hatred of Blacks diminished their own humanity. Thus the legacy of racism left the entire nation deficient of the basic human qualities on which it was supposedly founded. ❞
>
> Professor Sandra L. Barnes, Vanderbilt University

was a mature work, establishing the author as a serious national and international scholar.

True to his lifelong-held philosophy that researchers should apply their science to bring about social change, Du Bois left Atlanta University in 1910 to lead the National Association for the Advancement of Colored Peoples (NAACP).*

In 1920, he published *Darkwater: Voices from within the Veil*, the first of his three autobiographies. This dealt with the oppression of blacks globally and included a chapter on the resistance and struggles of black women in particular. By now, Du Bois's vision was pan-African,* universal even, encouraging minority struggles against oppression everywhere.

Black Reconstruction in America followed in 1935, looking at different economic classes during the period of Reconstruction.* It argued that the failure of white and black workers to unite against oppressive white property owners allowed the Jim Crow* laws to come about, disenfranchising most blacks *and* many poor whites in the late nineteenth and early twentieth centuries. This challenged the dominant idea that blacks were responsible for their own misfortunes. In this work, Du Bois also demonstrated how black resistance defied the Jim Crow laws and advanced overall humanity in the United States.

In 1950, Du Bois ran for the US Senate to represent New York, campaigning on the position that capitalism* was responsible for racism across the globe. Although Du Bois recognized that the Soviet Union* had many faults, he defended its political structure of communism* as a potential solution. He was not elected. In 1951 the American government put Du Bois on trial for his growing radicalism and prevented him from travelling abroad until 1958. In an act of defiance he joined the American Communist Party in 1961 and two years later moved to Ghana, a former British colony that had just gained independence. He became a Ghanaian citizen and continued his struggle against global racism from West Africa.

Integration

As a scholar, journalist and activist, Du Bois made a lifelong commitment to challenge racism and inequality and to advance the position of blacks in American society. His first seminal work, *The Philadelphia Negro*, written in 1899, provided him with deep insight into the challenges that blacks faced in their pursuit of equality. As he put it, "Merely being born into a group does not necessarily make one possessed of complete knowledge concerning it."[2] He lived among disenfranchised blacks in the American south and became a researcher and teacher on many different aspects of African American life.

Although he was not yet well acquainted with Marxism* when he wrote *Souls* in 1903, Du Bois nonetheless analyzes the political economy of racism and discusses it as a by-product of capitalism. He also addresses the effects racism has had on the formation of both black and white identities. Du Bois diagnoses "the color line" as the great divider of the twentieth century and introduces his seminal concepts of "double consciousness" and "the veil." Furthermore, he stresses the importance of education and leadership in attaining equal citizenship.

By the time of *Black Reconstruction*, which he wrote 32 years later in 1935, Du Bois had acquired a thorough knowledge of Marxism and he explores the relationship between the industrial economy and racism in some depth. Against the backdrop of the Great Depression*—the worldwide economic depression that lasted from 1929–39—he describes in detail how industrial capitalism creates a system that favors white property-owners over workers, and how racism is a tool the privileged classes use to expand their wealth. He also challenges the dominant idea that the proper emancipation of black people failed during the period of Reconstruction* because blacks were unsuccessful in politics and other areas of society. He argues that, contrary to popular belief, the north was not "the magnanimous emancipator" following the Civil War* and the south was not "a martyr to inescapable fate."[3] Du Bois identifies slavery as the primary cause of the Civil War and the Jim Crow laws that followed as a system that whites knowingly imposed on blacks to safeguard their own interests.

It is evident that Du Bois became more radical over time in response to key world events such as the Russian Revolution,* and the Cold War,* as well as his own experience of racism and inequality. But his entire body of work is united by his struggle for greater democracy and humanity.

Significance

During the course of Du Bois's life he made immense contributions to academia and society. He wrote 21 books, edited 15 more and published over 100 essays and articles.[4] He was also a leader of black civil-rights group the Niagara Movement,* the NAACP, and pan-Africanism, an ideology that encouraged the solidarity of Africans worldwide. *The Souls of Black Folk* was just one important contribution in his lifelong struggle for equality.

Although Du Bois's scholarship is usually associated with sociology it is, in fact, interdisciplinary, covering more than one academic subject. At an American Academy of Political and Social Sciences meeting in 1897 he argued that it was necessary to study "African American problems" in different dimensions by combining historical research, data analysis, anthropological measurement—data taken directly from people about the way they live—and sociological interpretation. Having done exactly that, Du Bois's scholarship has influenced sociology, history, economics, politics, religious studies, art and literature.

At present Du Bois's scholarship lies at the intersection of African American studies, race and ethnicity studies and post-colonial studies. Important scholars like Paul Gilroy* and Homi K. Bhabha* have revived his ideas about racism and black identity and have applied them to a much broader global context in response to anti-colonial struggles, decolonization (or the undoing of colonialism) and post-colonial immigration. The author's ideas are still important in academia, as well as continuing to inspire social movements globally.

NOTES

1   David Levering Lewis, *W. E. B. Du Bois: Biography of a Race, 1868–1919* (New York: Henry Holt, 1993), 191.

2   W. E. B. Du Bois, *The Autobiography of W. E. B. Du Bois*, (New York: International Publishers, 1968),198.

3   W. E. B. Du Bois, *Black Reconstruction in America* (New York: Russell and Russell, 1963), 723.

4   NAACP History: W. E. B. Du Bois, accessed January 28, 2015, http://www.naacp.org/pages/naacp-history-w.e.b.-dubois.

SECTION 3
IMPACT

THE FIRST RESPONSES

KEY POINTS

- Some anonymous reviewers praised *The Souls of Black Folk* for its great literary and social value. Others expressed mixed feelings. Still more claimed it was a dangerous book because it would ignite further racial tension.

- In 1904, a year after its publication, W. E. B. Du Bois acknowledged that *Souls* had some minor flaws. But he stood by all of the views he had expressed in the book.

- The most important factor that shaped the way people felt about the text was the period when it was written: namely the time of the Jim Crow* laws.*

Criticism

W. E. B. Du Bois's *The Souls of Black Folk* posed a bold challenge to the dominant idea that blacks were biologically and culturally inferior to whites and were responsible for their own failed emancipation during Reconstruction.* Like other Du Bois works, it used powerful and persuasive arguments to show how far from the truth this was.

The immediate response after publication was mixed. On the one hand, some praised *Souls* for its literary and social brilliance, such as one anonymous reviewer from *The Nation* magazine who expressed his awe over the emotional power of the text and its ability to captivate the reader. Another from the *Methodist Magazine and Review* commented on Du Bois's "fine literary grace," while a reviewer from *The Westminster Review* argued that "the work offers a rational solution to the colour problem that has so long perplexed the United States."[1]

On the other hand, some viewed the book as threatening, claiming

> ❝ If Du Bois sincerely feared, as he suggested in 'The After-Thought,' that his book might fall 'still-born into the world wilderness,' reassurance came quickly. ❞
> Professor David Levering Lewis, New York University

it would ignite further racial tension. One anonymous reviewer in the *Nashville American* wrote, "This book is indeed dangerous for the Negro to read, for it will only excite discontent and race hatred and fill his imagination with things that do not exist, or things that should not bear upon his mind." Another anonymous reviewer from the *New York Times* criticized Du Bois for attacking Booker T. Washington* and argued that, as a northern black, Du Bois should not be speaking for the American south.[2]

Other critics were ambivalent. An anonymous reviewer from the *American Monthly Review of Reviews* wrote, "No book of similar character has been printed in recent years that equals this little volume in power or grace of expression," but then argued that "as a practical solution for the educational problem of the black race, his essays cannot be regarded as of equal value with the widely published lectures and addresses of Mr. Washington."[3]

Responses
In 1904 Du Bois published a review of his own work in *The Independent* journal. Although he did not respond directly to criticisms, he did reflect on *Souls* in retrospect. He apologized for the abruptness of certain sections of the text, explaining that since he had written it over the course of seven years he had mixed different styles, tones and ideas. Nevertheless, in conclusion Du Bois stood by his arguments and made it clear that what connected all 14 essays was the idea that America *was* a deeply racist nation and that this racism must be overcome.[4]

The debate between Du Bois and Washington over the direction blacks should take against racism and inequality persisted until Washington's death in 1915. Du Bois continued to argue that only education, leadership, resistance and struggle would bring about equality in American society. In particular, he stressed the need for highly educated blacks like himself to guide the masses in transforming society. While Du Bois's view became more radical over time, the essence of his work was consistent from beginning to end.

Conflict And Consensus

The historical period in which Du Bois published *Souls* shaped its reception. Although some radicals praised Du Bois for his literary and social brilliance, many white southerners criticized him for challenging the status quo, an existing state of affairs that privileged whites and allowed them to expand their wealth.[5]

White southerners saw black political speaker Booker T. Washington as an ally because he was prepared to accommodate the idea that whites were naturally superior and that blacks should submit to them. As a presidential advisor, Washington had some financial control over black education and enjoyed a good reputation among powerful whites, who thought of him as someone who would help them make it acceptable to continue exploiting blacks.

Du Bois referred to Washington's way of dealing with racism as the Tuskegee Machine. Tuskegee in Alabama was where Washington had built a black college as he tried to improve the lot of African Americans. Du Bois did not agree with Washington's belief that cooperation with whites was the way to defeat racism but he recognized that it was very difficult to bring down Washington's stronghold. As Du Bois put it: "Most of the papers found it to their advantage certainly not to oppose Mr. Washington, even if they did not wholly agree with him. Negroes who sought high positions groveled for his favor."[6]

Nevertheless, through his writings, teaching and activism, Du Bois did challenge Washington's position as the leading black intellectual of the time. With his persuasive and scientifically based arguments he managed to make some whites reflect on the situation in America and provide inspiration and impetus for the advancement of blacks in America and elsewhere.

NOTES

1　W. E. B. Du Bois, *The Souls of Black Folk* (New York and London: W.W. Norton and Company, 1999), xx, 221–234.

2　Du Bois, *The Souls of Black Folk*, 26.

3　Albert Shaw, "The New Books: Notes on Recent American Publications," *American Monthly Review of Reviews* 28 (1903): 249.

4　W. E. B. Du Bois, "The Souls of Black Folk," *The Independent* 57 (1904): 2920.

5　Du Bois, *The Souls of Black Folk*, 221–234.

6　W. E. B. Du Bois, *Dusk of Dawn: Essay Towards an Autobiography of a Race* (New York: Harcourt Brace, 1940), 76.

MODULE 10
THE EVOLVING DEBATE

KEY POINTS

- *The Souls of Black Folk* and W. E. B. Du Bois's wider body of work give a detailed analysis of racism in the America of the Jim Crow* laws, encouraging the struggle for equality. This has had a major impact, both in the United States and elsewhere.

- Today Du Bois's legacy lies at the crossroads of black political thought, race and ethnicity studies and post-colonial studies.

- His scholarship has shaped the ideas of prominent scholars such as Paul Gilroy* and Homi K. Bhabha.* Both have extended his concept of "double consciousness" by applying it to post-colonial research.

Uses And Problems

The three key concepts of W. E. B. Du Bois's *The Souls of Black Folk* are "the color line," "double consciousness," and "the veil."

During the course of his life Du Bois's view of "the color line" changed. Whereas in 1903 he portrays it quite narrowly as a marker of division between whites and blacks, in "*The Negro and the Warsaw Ghetto*"[1] in 1952 he explains that he did not fully understand the condition of blacks in the United States until he witnessed how Jews lived in the Warsaw Ghetto* during World War II.* As Du Bois puts it:

"The problem of slavery, emancipation and caste in the United States was no longer in my mind a separate and unique thing as I had long conceived it. It was not even solely a matter of color and physical and racial characteristics … No, the race problem in which I was

> ❝ Although our society is more tolerant than ever before, a new form of racism exists – aversive racism – characterized by egalitarian attitudes, but avoidance and subtle discrimination against Blacks. And Blacks continue to face the dilemma of double consciousness. As posited by Cornel West (1993), research confirms that 'race' still matters in terms of opportunity, access, treatment, and quality of life. ❞
>
> Professor Sandra L. Barnes, Vanderbilt University

interested cut across lines of color and physique and belief and status and was a matter of cultural patterns, perverted teaching and human hate and prejudice, which reached all sorts of people and caused endless evil to all men."[2]

This quote is important because it shows how Du Bois came to understand that racism was more than just a "veil" separating whites and blacks in America. Instead, it shows his understanding of racism as an ever-changing phenomenon that adapts across time. Since then, a wide variety of scholars ranging from Hannah Arendt* to Paul Gilroy have studied the nature of racism and its relationship to other forms of discrimination, such as anti-Semitism* and gender discrimination.

Du Bois first used the term "double consciousness" in 1897's *"Strivings of the Negro People."* He then developed it further in *Souls*. It refers to the identity conflict in being both African and American in a profoundly racist society. As Du Bois observes, "[The African American] simply wishes to make it possible for a man to be both a Negro and an American without being cursed and spit upon by his fellows, without having the doors of opportunity closed roughly in his face."[3]

Du Bois uses the term "the veil" as a metaphor to describe the division between these two consciousnesses (the African and the

American) and two societies (white and black). He believes this "color line" is both a curse and a blessing, a danger that can be overcome through struggle and recognition.

Different scholars have applied Du Bois's metaphor of "the color line" and "the veil" to other contexts. One prominent example is Martinique-born African-French writer and revolutionary Frantz Fanon,*who used these concepts in his seminal 1952 work *Black Skin, White Masks* to describe black identity as it is understood by white colonialists. In one passage Fanon describes a young white boy who sees Fanon, points at him and says, "Look, a Negro!" He then jumps in his mother's arms looking for safety. Experiencing this, Fanon feels a painful denial of his own identity. He says, "My body was given back to me sprawled out, distorted, recolored, clad in mourning in that white winter day."[4]

This passage is similar to Du Bois's first encounter with blackness, when he offers a greeting card to a white girl at Fisk University and she refuses to accept it. Du Bois describes his experience as follows:

"Then it dawned upon me with a certain suddenness that I was different from the others; or like [them perhaps] in heart and life and longing, but shut out from their world by a vast veil."[5]

Schools Of Thought

In 1903, Du Bois belonged to two schools of thought. First, he made a major contribution to the development of sociology as an evidence-based discipline. He did this by explaining the material causes of racism against the backdrop of the Jim Crow* laws and how this led to inequality. Second, by opposing Booker T. Washington* and defending social struggle and equality, Du Bois carried on the tradition of those who had fought against slavery like Frederick Douglass.* Du Bois was an integrationist, which means he believed that, by means of social conflict, white and black society could eventually be united into one multicultural unit where democracy and humanity would flourish. In this sense he was a precursor to Martin Luther King,* but found himself at odds with the separatist view of Marcus Garvey,* who set the stage for the Black Power* movement of the 1960s which advocated black separatism.

Today Du Bois's work sits at the intersection of black political thought, race and ethnicity studies and post-colonial studies. His entire body of work focuses on racism and how the oppressed can transcend "the color line." His late works, such as 1961's *Worlds of Color*, move beyond the borders of the United States by calling for the end of colonial domination and global imperialism, which Du Bois associated closely with capitalism.*

In Current Scholarship

Du Bois has influenced many current scholars, in particular Paul Gilroy and Homi K. Bhabha. In his work *The Black Atlantic*, Gilroy extends Du Bois's description of "double consciousness" to people of African descent everywhere. He focuses on how these people have simultaneously been an integral part of history and yet have been violently excluded from that history. He says that they have made immense scientific, literary, political, social and cultural contributions to society and yet whites have cast them as inferior and not allowed them the freedoms of whites or full citizenship. Black intellectuals today are in a position to question injustice and are invested with what Gilroy calls "a special clarity of vision" or "a dreadful objectivity." These black intellectual voices have struggled against racism in the United States and against European colonialism and have successfully questioned the dominant argument of "rational, western progress"— the idea that white western culture is naturally superior.[6]

In *The Location of Culture*, Homi K. Bhabha also builds on Du Bois's concept of "double consciousness" by arguing that a Third Space has emerged where individuals have evolving identities made up of more than one background or culture. This moves beyond the two-part vision put forward by Du Bois, where you are black or white and nothing in between. Bhabha argues that a disruption of these strict barriers means there is an ongoing interchange between the "colonizer" and the "colonized" that can ultimately lead to progress and greater humanity.

NOTES

1   W. E. B. Du Bois, "The Negro and the Warsaw Ghetto," *Jewish Life* (May 1952).

2   W. E. B. Du Bois, "Social Theory of W. E. B. Du Bois, The Negro and the Warsaw Ghetto," in Phil Zuckerman, *Jewish Life* (Thousand Oaks: Pine Forge Press, 2004), 45–46.

3   W. E. B. Du Bois, *The Souls of Black Folk* (New York and London: W.W. Norton and Company, 1999), 10–11.

4   Frantz Fanon, *Black Skins, White Masks* (London: MacGibbon and Kee, 1968), 113.

5   Du Bois, *The Souls of Black Folk*, 10.

6   Paul Gilroy, *The Black Atlantic: Modernity and Double Consciousness* (London: Verso, 1993), 29, 38–9, 171.

MODULE 11
IMPACT AND INFLUENCE TODAY

KEY POINTS

- *Souls* remains a seminal text within a variety of academic disciplines.
- The text continues to challenge racism and inequalities and to encourage struggle against them.
- Broadly speaking, the book now challenges anyone who is racist or holds a non-critical stance on racism.

Position

In 1999 and 2003 there were commemorations of the 100-year anniversaries of W. E. B. Du Bois's *The Philadelphia Negro*[1] and *The Souls of Black Folk*[2] respectively. In 2005 there were centennial celebrations of black civil rights organization the Niagara Movement,[*3] which Du Bois founded in 1905. Additionally, in 2009 President Barack Obama delivered an address at the 100-year commemoration of the National Association for the Advancement of Colored People (NAACP),[4] which Du Bois co-founded. These milestone celebrations were accompanied by a number of academic journal and book publications,[5] as well as media coverage from newspapers and magazines such as the *New York Times.*[6] All this highlighted the extent to which Du Bois is still very much part of, and indeed an inspiration for, discussions on race, racism, identity, democracy, equality and human rights.

In 2003, the National Black Arts Festival in Atlanta commemorated music, drama and other arts inspired by Du Bois.[7] In the same year at City University of New York's Graduate Center, renowned playwright

> **❝** The 'duality' of African Americans—their double-
> consciousness—became a signal contribution to the
> notion of the fragmentation of the self, a defining
> condition of modernism. The once audacious idea that all
> identities are multiple is now a commonplace ... Delving
> into the particular to speak to the universal is what, of
> course, a classic does. Through his curiously powerful
> text, the particularity of the Negro became a metaphor,
> a universal aspect of the human condition. And because
> of this, *The Souls of Black Folk* continues to speak so
> compellingly to a new generation of readers today. **❞**
> Professor Henry Louis Gates Jr., Harvard University

Thulani Davis* led dramatic readings of different passages of *The Souls of Black Folk* featuring prominent figures, like the actor Danny Glover.[8] There is clearly very strong current interest in reviving and revisiting Du Bois's work.

Interaction

When *Souls* was first published in 1903 Du Bois posed a challenge to white supremacy and to Booker T. Washington* and his supporters' accommodationist stance. Broadly speaking, the book today challenges anyone who is racist or holds a non-critical stance on racism. Du Bois believed that racism was a social construction put in place by whites for their own material gain. Examples of non-critical stances include: claims that "multiculturalism" is responsible for social breakdown; the failure to account for the root causes of riots; claims that ethnic minorities are to blame for the discrimination they face; and assertions that Western societies have advanced to a point that they are "post-racial" and ideas of differences between the way races are treated are no longer relevant.

The book is still an important reference point for academics, journalists, and activists who want to understand and explain a number of issues:

- The causes of racism
- How racism shapes identity
- Inequality
- The importance of minority education and leadership
- The role of religion and spirituality in fostering collective resistance
- The legacies of minority struggles globally

The Continuing Debate

Today, Du Bois is still a major influence for scholars of race and ethnicity studies and for post-colonial research. "The color line," "double consciousness," and "the veil" remain important themes in these fields. Psychology professors John F. Dovidio* and Samuel L. Gaertner,* for example, have addressed how discussions about racism have changed since Du Bois published *Souls*. They point to the way racism has become more subtle in the West and is frequently camouflaged by talk of multiculturalism, anti-racism, and egalitarianism.[9]

American sociologist E. Franklin Frazier,* who is also an author on racism, has shown how the equivalent of the rural cabins described by Du Bois as "dirty and dilapidated, smelling of eating and sleeping, poorly ventilated, and anything but homes"[10] are today urban slums characterized by segregation, squalor, and lack of opportunity.[11]

Other scholars such as Douglas Massey* and Nancy Denton* have shown that color-based racism persists to this day, particularly when it comes to the amount of discrimination faced by blacks in the fields of education and employment in modern-day United States. They have argued for economic reform to address a growing sense of angst among lower-class African Americans.[12] American philosopher and public intellectual Cornel West* has asked: why are there so few prominent black leaders such as Du Bois today?[13]

Scholars such as African–American studies expert Andrew Billingsley*[14] and the activist Eric Lincoln*[15] have pointed to the importance of religion in *Souls* and the book's emphasis on striving for greater spiritual humanity. Both feel this is an area of the work that has been overlooked. They highlight the historical role of the black Church as a provider of education, economic aid, and sanctuary and solidarity against racism, gangs, drugs, and poverty. They also highlight the important role of the black church in helping to create black leaders such as Martin Luther King.* All of this shows how the central themes of *Souls* remain relevant in modern scholarship.

NOTES

1   See, for example: Lynn Burbridge, "W. E. B. Du Bois as Economic Analyst: Reflections on the 100th Year Anniversary of The Philadelphia Negro," *Review of Black Political Economy* 26, no. 3 (1999): 13–31.

2   There are too many examples to cite here. Commemoration events took place across the United States.

3   See, for example, Patricia Donovan, "Event to Mark Centennial of Niagara Movement," *University of Buffalo Reporter*, July 7, 2005, accessed January 29, 2015, http://www.buffalo.edu/ubreporter/archive/vol36/vol36n41/articles/NiagaraMovement.html?print=1.

4   "Remarks by the President to the NAACP Centennial Convention," The White House, Office of the Press Secretary, July 17, 2009, accessed January 28, 2015, http://www.whitehouse.gov/the-press-office/remarks-president-naacp-centennial-convention-07162009.

5   See, for example: Dolan Hubbard, *The Souls of Black Folk: 100 Years Later* (Columbia: University of Missouri Press, 2007).

6   Henry Louis Gates Jr., "The Souls of Black Folk at 100: Both Sides Now," *New York Times*, May 4, 2003, accessed January 28, 2015, http://www.nytimes.com/2003/05/04/books/review/04GATEST.html.

7   TaRessa Stovall, "Arts Festival Celebrates W. E. B. Du Bois and the Diaspora," *The Crisis* 110, no. 5 (2003): 48.

8 Press Release: "'Souls of Black Folk: A Centennial Celebration' To Premiere at Graduate Center Stars Featured in Dramatic Readings of Du Bois's Classic Work," January 1, 2003, accessed January 28, 2015, http://www.gc.cuny.edu/News/GC-News/Detail?id=5920.

9 John F. Dovidio and Samuel L. Gaertner, "The Aversive Forms of Racism," in *Prejudice, Discrimination, and Racism,* eds. John F. Dovidio and Samuel L. Gaertner (Orlando: Academic Press, 1986), 61–89.

10 Du Bois, *The Souls of Black Folk*, 91.

11 E. Franklin Frazier, *The Negro Church in America* (Liverpool: Liverpool University Press, 1964).

12 Douglas Massey and Nancy Denton, *American Apartheid: Segregation and the Making of the Underclass* (Massachusetts: Harvard University Press, 1993).

13 Cornel West, "The Dilemma of the Black Intellectual," *Critical Quarterly* 29, no.4 (1987): 39–52.

14 Andrew Billingsley, *Mighty Like a River: The Black Church and Social Reform* (New York: Oxford University Press, 1999).

15 Eric Lincoln, *Race, Religion and the Continuing American Dilemma* (New York: Hill and Wang, 1984).

WHERE NEXT?

KEY POINTS

- *The Souls of Black Folk* will most likely continue to influence black studies, race and ethnicity studies, and post-colonial studies. It appears W. E. B. Du Bois will remain an important inspiration for social movements globally.

- Du Bois's core concepts—"the color line," "double consciousness," and "the veil"—will probably continue to serve as important reference points for further research.

- The text is seminal because it improves our understanding of racism, how it affects identity, and how we can collectively struggle to overcome it.

Potential

There were large-scale 100-year commemorations of *The Souls of Black Folk* in 2003 and there are strong links in modern scholarship between W. E. B. Du Bois's work and race and ethnicity studies, as well as post-colonial studies. This suggests that this text in particular and Du Bois's wider body of work will continue to be important in the future. His insights on racism in America, its origins in the world of making money, its impact on identity, and the author's hope that America will one day transform "the color line" in order to become truly democratic and achieve greater humanity are timeless, despite being rooted in a particular context of United States history, specifically the Jim Crow* laws. These core issues not only remain relevant in the United States today, but they also apply more broadly. In the future, scholars are likely to continue linking Du Bois to the historical discrimination and inequalities faced by blacks and other minorities,

> 66 Du Bois understood how change would come—just as [Martin Luther] King★ and all the civil rights giants did later. They understood that unjust laws needed to be overturned; that legislation needed to be passed; and that Presidents needed to be pressured into action. They knew that the stain of slavery and the sin of segregation had to be lifted in the courtroom and in the legislature. But they also knew that here, in America, change would have to come from the people ... Because of what they did, we are a more perfect union. 99
>
> Barack Obama, President of the United States

and their struggles to overcome them.

Although *Souls* refers specifically to an American context, Du Bois's later work, ending with the novel *Dark Princess* in 1928, addresses his pan-African★ vision of equality. As he puts it, "Africa is, of course, my fatherland ... one thing is sure and that is the fact that since the fifteenth century these ancestors of mine have had a common history, have suffered a common disaster, and have one long memory ... the badge of color is relatively unimportant save as a badge; the real essence of its kinship is the heritage of slavery; the discrimination and insult ... it is this unity that draws me to Africa."[1]

Future Directions

Although social movements have made much progress over time, "the color line" remains a major problem in the twenty-first century, even if its nature changes along with political, economic, social, and cultural transformations. Today, racism in America is characterized by the connections between such elements as class, skin color, religion, and gender. As Du Bois made clear when he saw the conditions of Jews in the Warsaw ghetto★ during World War II,★ racism is a much broader and more complex phenomenon than the one he depicted in his earlier works. Through his own personal journey from Great Barrington, Massachusetts, to Ghana his outlook matured and he came to understand the various dimensions of racism much better. In the future, this theme and its links with the formation of identity, human rights, resistance, struggle, and negotiation will likely continue to be explored by students, scholars, journalists, and activists. Those who study race and ethnicity, and post-colonialism such as Paul Gilroy* and Homi K. Bhabha,* are examples. However, the text is interdisciplinary, affecting different academic fields of study, and could benefit from greater attention from other fields such as religious studies.

Summary

The Souls of Black Folk is an essential read for anyone who wants to understand American and African-American history better. Du Bois built on the legacy of the former slave Frederick Douglass* by providing a detailed, scientifically based analysis of slavery, the American Civil War,* the Emancipation Proclamation,* the Reconstruction* era, and Jim Crow* discrimination. Despite having the right to vote and having been awarded other important freedoms in the Thirteenth, Fourteenth, and Fifteenth Amendments to the Constitution,* these Jim Crow laws ultimately re-enslaved blacks.

The text also provides significant insight into the social construction of race as a means to advance white economic interests and challenges the dominant argument of the times that blacks were biologically and culturally inferior to whites. It also details the effects of racism on black identity.

Throughout *Souls,* Du Bois aims to be the new leader of "the Negro cause" by urging blacks to be proud of their culture and to draw from their spirituality. He drives black people to engage collectively in social struggle so that whites will acknowledge their past injustices and recognize blacks as equals. Du Bois hopes that by this means African Americans will eventually be able to lift "the veil," overcome the tormenting condition of "double consciousness," and help whites make America the great democracy it claims to be—that is, "one nation, indivisible, under God."

It is likely that the book's three most important concepts—"the color line," "double consciousness," and "the veil"— will remain fundamental for a long time to come, not just in sociology, but in many fields ranging from anthropology to history to economics to politics. The book will probably also remain at the heart of race and ethnicity studies and postcolonial analyses, the main reason being that racism—against a backdrop of capitalism—continues to exist and affect identity. It can only be overcome—as Du Bois so persuasively argued in 1903—through education, leadership, and social conflict. The issues may have changed, subtly or otherwise, but the "color line" continues to be very much a problem of the twenty-first century.

NOTES

1   W. E. B. Du Bois, *Dusk of Dawn: Essay Towards an Autobiography of a Race* (New York: Harcourt Brace, 1940), 116.

GLOSSARY

GLOSSARY OF TERMS

Abolition: refers to the end of slavery in the United States.

Abolitionist Movement: refers to the movement before the American Civil War to end slavery.

American Civil War: a war fought in the United States between northern (Union) and southern (Confederate) states from 1861 to 1865.

Anti-Semitism: prejudice or hostility towards Jews.

Atlanta Compromise: an agreement made in Atlanta in 1895 that established that blacks would submit to white racism and political rule in exchange for basic legal rights and a basic education.

Atlantic Monthly: founded in Boston in 1857, this is one of the oldest and most respected magazines in the United States.

Black is Beautiful: a cultural movement that began in the United States in the 1960s which sought to dispel the myth that black physical features were less beautiful than white ones.

Black Codes: laws passed in former confederate states to restrict the activity of freed black and ensure their availability as a labour force following the abolition of slavery.

Black Nationalism: the idea that blacks should separate from white society and govern themselves.

Black Power: a political movement that began in the United States in the 1960s that encouraged black separatism.

Capitalism: an economic system that emphasizes the private ownership of the means of production. Du Bois argued that there was a strong link between capitalism and racism.

Civilizing Mission: the doctrine upon which European colonialism operated, justifying exploitation in the colonies by claiming Europe had been given the duty to civilize "the uncivilized."

Cold War: the state of political hostility that existed between the Soviet bloc (Russia and its allies) and the West from 1945 to 1990.

Communism: a political ideology that relies on the state ownership of the means of production, the collectivization of labor, and the abolition of social class.

Congress: the national legislative body of the United States, comprised of the Senate and the House of Representatives. Congress passed the Fifteenth Amendment in 1870, granting African Americans the right to vote.

Consciousness: according to Hegel, consciousness is the awareness of another's awareness of oneself. In other words, we see ourselves through the eyes of others.

Constitution: a set of principles upon which a state is recognized to be founded. The US Constitution, signed in 1787, replaced the Articles of Confederation with a stronger central government.

Declaration of the Rights of Man and of the Citizen: a document signed by the French National Constituent Assembly in

1789. It stresses that all men are naturally equal, and thus have equal rights under the law.

Elegy: a poem of mourning and reverence.

Emancipation Proclamation: a political proclamation made by President Abraham Lincoln in 1863 in the middle of the Civil War. It established that all persons held as slaves in the rebellious southern states would be free from that moment on.

Enlightenment: a cultural and intellectual movement in the seventeenth and eighteenth centuries that looked to reform society through the use of reason. This provided the "scientific" backdrop for the work of Herbert Spencer and Charles Darwin, who argued that blacks were biologically and culturally inferior to whites.

Evolutionary Biology: a field of academic inquiry concerned with the evolutionary processes that produce the diversity of life on Earth. When W. E. B. Du Bois published *Souls*, the dominant view in the social sciences was that blacks were biologically inferior to whites.

Freedman's Bureau: a federal agency from 1865 to 1872 that integrated freed slaves by providing them with educational services, legal counsel, and employment aid.

French Revolution: a period of political and social upheaval in France that began in 1789 with the popular overthrow of the monarchy and ended in 1799 with the rise of Napoleon.

Great Depression: the global financial crisis that began in 1929 and continued until World War II.

Great Man Theory: a theory which argues that great men use their intelligence, wisdom, charisma, and political acumen to transform history.

Jim Crow Laws: a period in American history from the end of Reconstruction in1877 until the civil rights movements of the 1950s and 1960s. State and federal governments put a number of laws in place to stop blacks from attaining greater equality. Du Bois published *The Souls of Black Folk* during this era.

Ku Klux Klan: a secret society founded in the United States in 1866 that reasserted white supremacy through violence.

Literacy Test: a test used during the period of Jim Crow by some states and local governments as part of the voting registration process for blacks. Those who could not read or could not pass the test were denied their right to vote, as allowed in the Fifteenth Amendment.

Marxism: the name given to the political system advocated by Karl Marx. It emphasised an end to capitalism by taking control of the means of production from individuals and placing it in the hands of central government.

National Association for the Advancement of Colored People (NAACP): a black civil rights organization formed by W. E. B. Du Bois, Moorfield Storey and Mary White Ovington in 1909. It worked to end racism and achieve equality.

Naturalist: a person who studies or is an expert in natural history, for example Charles Darwin. His views were very influential when W. E. B. Du Bois published *Souls*.

Niagara Movement: a black civil rights organization founded by W. E. B. Du Bois and William Monroe Trotter in 1905. It opposed the accommodationist stance of Booker T. Washington, and called for an end to racial segregation.

On the Origin of Species: a seminal work published in 1859 by naturalist Charles Darwin. It is widely considered to be the foundation of evolutionary biology, which shaped the dominant view when W. E. B. Du Bois published *Souls* that blacks were biologically inferior to whites.

Pan-Africanism: the idea that all people of African descent have common interests and should unite.

Plessy versus Ferguson: a landmark court case in the United States in 1896 that upheld the right of state and local governments to practice segregation under the doctrine of "separate but equal."

Poll Taxes: a tax levied as a prerequisite for voting. During the period of Jim Crow some states and local governments implemented a tax, which prevented blacks who couldn't or didn't want to pay it from exercising their right to vote, as stipulated in the Fifteenth Amendment.

Protestant: a Christian whose faith and practice are founded on the principles of the Reformation. W. E. B. Du Bois had a Protestant upbringing.

Reconstruction: the period from 1865 to 1877 when the federal government of the United States reincorporated the southern states into the Union.

Russian Revolution: a series of revolutions in Russia in 1917 that destroyed the Tsar's ruling authority and led to the creation of the Soviet Union. Du Bois studied the Russian Revolution and travelled to Russia in 1927.

Scientific Method: a method of investigation whereby a problem is first identified and observations and experiments are then carried out to construct ways to solve it. W. E. B. Du Bois applied the scientific method to his seminal works.

Soviet Union: a federal communist republic officially known as the Union of Soviet Socialist Republics that existed between 1922 and 1991.

Talented Tenth: a term used by Du Bois to refer to a well-educated elite group of black leaders who could lead the masses in their struggle for equality. It is based on the assumption that one in 10 black people could become such leaders.

Universal Negro Improvement Association: a fraternal association founded in 1914 that aimed to encourage solidarity among blacks so that they could separate from white society and govern themselves.

Valley of the Shadow of Death: a phrase used in Psalm 23:4 of the Bible. It refers to a situation of grave danger, in which hope still exists if one fears no evil. Du Bois believed that although blacks suffer great discrimination, their resistance and struggle would eventually lead them to overcome prejudice.

Vietnam War: a military conflict (1955–75) between South Vietnam—supported by the United States—and Communist North

Vietnam. Du Bois's communist vision of society in the late stage of his life was shaped by Cold War events, including the Vietnam War.

Warsaw Ghetto: the largest of the Jewish ghettoes in occupied Europe during World War II.

World War II (1939–45): global war between the vast majority of world states, including all the great powers of the time.

PEOPLE MENTIONED IN THE TEXT

Hannah Arendt (1906–75) was one of the most famous political theorists of the twentieth century. She was staunchly anti-totalitarian and supportive of freedom and analyzed the relationship between different forms of discrimination.

Aristotle (384–322 b.c.e) was an ancient Greek philosopher whose ideas were one of the inspirations for the modern development of the social sciences, including sociology.

Homi K. Bhabha (b. 1949) is Anne F. Rothenberg Professor of English and American Literature and Language, and the Director of the Humanities Center at Harvard University. In his work *The Location of Culture*, Bhabha extended Du Bois's ideas about double-consciousness to argue that in the postcolonial era there is a Third Space of people who exist between "the colonizer" and "the colonized."

Andrew Billingsley is a sociologist and renowned scholar of black studies at the University of South Carolina. He has argued that *Souls* provides great insight into black spirituality, which he claims has been largely overlooked in scholarly literature.

Thomas Carlyle (1795–1881) was a Scottish philosopher and historian. His book *On Heroes, Hero-Worship, and the Heroic in History* argued that great men transform history through their intelligence, wisdom, charisma, and political acumen.

Auguste Comte (1798–1857) was a French philosopher, the founder of sociology and the doctrine of positivism which argues that knowledge can be scientifically tested.

Charles Darwin (1809–82) was a British naturalist and geologist considered to be the father of the evolutionary theory, which challenged the idea that God created the universe.

Thulani Davis (b. 1949) is a well-known American writer and playwright. She has performed dramatic readings of W. E. B. Du Bois's writings in theaters in the United States.

Nancy Denton is a professor of sociology at the University of Albany, who has published work on segregation in the United States, including *American Apartheid*. She has highlighted the importance of *Souls* with regard to racism and black identity, and claims that racism is still a major problem in American society.

Frederick Douglass (1818–95) was an escaped slave who became a writer, orator, statesman, and leader in the abolitionist movement to outlaw slavery in the United States.

John F. Dovidio is a professor of psychology at Yale University. He argues that the discourse of racism has changed since W. E. B. Du Bois published *Souls*; he claims that racism today is more subtle, and is codified as multiculturalism, anti-racism, and egalitarianism.

Emile Durkheim (1858–1917) was a French sociologist and one of the principal architects of modern social science. He advocated the application of the scientific method to social analysis and established the first European department of sociology at the University of Bordeaux in 1895.

Ralph Waldo Emerson (1803–82) was a well-known American

writer and philosopher of the nineteenth century who championed transcendentalism or the idea that philosophy and literature should challenge the current state of society and culture. In his work he coined the term "double consciousness," though he did not relate it to African Americans, as Du Bois did.

Frantz Fanon (1925–61) was a Martinique-born Afro-French philosopher and revolutionary who wrote *The Wretched of the Earth* and *Black Skin, White Masks*. W. E. B. Du Bois influenced his work on racism and black identity.

E. Franklin Frazier (1894–1962) was an American sociologist and author who wrote many books on blacks in America, including *The Negro Family in the United States*. He has argued that the segregation, squalor, and lack of opportunity that W. E. B. Du Bois describes in *Souls* in rural areas now occurs in cities.

Samuel L. Gaertner is a professor of psychology at the University of Delaware. He argues that the discourse of racism has changed since W. E. B. Du Bois published *Souls*; he claims that today it is more subtle, and is codified as multiculturalism, anti-racism, and egalitarianism.

Marcus Garvey (1887–1940) was a Jamaican political leader who promoted the cause of Black Nationalism, in which whites and blacks would live in separate societies. He was the founder of the Black Star Line, which hoped to return all people of African descent to Africa.

Paul Gilroy (b. 1956) is a professor of American and English Literature at King's College London. Gilroy's *The Black Atlantic* extends the ideas of Du Bois by linking the lived experiences of racism of black people globally.

Ulysses Grant (1822–85) was an army general and president of the United States from 1869 to1877. He led the Union army to victory in the Civil War and was president during Reconstruction.

Georg Wilhelm Friedrich Hegel (1770–1831) was a German philosopher whose theories heavily influenced Karl Marx. In *Souls*, Du Bois adapted Hegel's link between history and consciousness in *The Phenomenology of the Spirit* to the condition of African Americans in the United States.

Henry James (1843–1916) was a well-known British-American writer who wrote *The Portrait of a Lady* and *The Turn of the Screw*. He praised W. E. B. Du Bois for his literary brilliance in *Souls*.

Rudyard Kipling (1865–1936) was an Indian-born English writer, one of the most popular in the nineteenth and twentieth centuries. He is the author of the poem "The White Man's Burden," in which he argues that colonialism is a noble mission because the white man has been given the responsibility of civilizing the black man.

Martin Luther King Jr. (1929–68) was a Baptist minister and activist who led the civil rights movements in the United States from the 1950s until his assassination in 1968. King built on the legacy of Du Bois, who had co-founded the Niagara Movement and the NAACP.

David Levering Lewis (b. 1936) is a professor of history at New York University who has won two Pulitzer prizes for his two-part biography of W. E. B. Du Bois.

Abraham Lincoln (1809–65) was president of the United States from 1861 until his assassination in 1865. He led the country through the Civil War and abolished slavery.

Eric Lincoln (1924–2000) was an African-American scholar who taught at several institutions in the United States, including Duke University. He argues that *Souls* provides great insight into black spirituality, which he claims has been largely overlooked in scholarly literature.

Karl Marx (1818–83) was a German philosopher, economist, historian and sociologist, widely considered one of history's most influential social scientists. Although Du Bois only had a basic understanding of Marxism when he wrote *Souls*, his later works such as *Black Reconstruction* reflect a much deeper understanding of the relationship between capitalism and racism.

Douglas Massey (b. 1952) is a professor of sociology at Princeton University. He has highlighted the importance of W. E. B. Du Bois's work, and has made clear in his own work that racism is still a major problem in American society.

Herbert Spencer (1820–1903) was an English philosopher, biologist and sociologist who was an important figure in the domain of evolutionary theory before Charles Darwin. He coined the term "the survival of the fittest."

Lester Ward (1841–1913) was the first president of the American Sociological Association and promoted the introduction of sociology courses into American higher education.

Booker T. Washington (1856–1915) was the most prominent black leader in America from 1890 to 1915. He argued that blacks should accept white racism and political rule in exchange for basic legal rights and a basic education, a position that W. E. B. Du Bois firmly opposed.

Max Weber (1864–1920) was a German philosopher, sociologist, and political economist who deeply influenced social theory, social research, and sociology. When Du Bois studied in Berlin he came into contact with Weber and studied his ideas.

Cornel West (b. 1953) was the first black PhD graduate in philosophy from Princeton University, and is a prominent intellectual in the United States today. He has highlighted the importance of W. E. B. Du Bois's work, and has asked: why are there so few black figures like Du Bois today?

Robert Wortham is a professor of sociology at North Carolina Central University. He argued that sociologists often overlook the great contributions of W. E. B. Du Bois.

Earl Wright is a professor of African studies at the University of Cincinnati. He is an expert on the scholarship of W. E. B. Du Bois.

Shamoon Zamir is a professor of literature and visual studies at New York University, Abu Dhabi. He has written a book entitled *Dark Voices: W. E. B. Du Bois and American Thought: 1888–1903*.

WORKS CITED

WORKS CITED

Aptheker, Herbert, ed. *The Correspondence of W. E. B. Du Bois: Volume III, Selections 1944–1963*. Amherst: University of Massachusetts Press, 1978.

Barnes, Sandra L. "A Sociological Examination of W. E. B. Du Bois' The Souls of Black Folk." *The North Star, A Journal of African American Religious History* 6 (2003): 2.

Billingsley, Andrew. *Mighty Like a River: The Black Church and Social Reform*. New York: Oxford University Press, 1999.

Burbridge, Lynn. "W. E. B. Du Bois as Economic Analyst: Reflections on the 100th Year Anniversary of the Philadelphia Negro." *The Review of Black Political Economy* 26, no. 3 (1999): 13–31.

Comte, Auguste. *Comte: Early Political Writings*. Edited by H.S. Jones. Cambridge: Cambridge University Press, 1998.

Darwin, Charles. *The Descent of Man*. London: John Murray, 1871.

Donovan, Patricia. "Event to Mark Centennial of Niagara Movement." *University of Buffalo Reporter*, July 7, 2005. Accessed January 29, 2015. http://www.buffalo.edu/ubreporter/archive/vol36/vol36n41/articles/NiagaraMovement.html?print=1.

Douglass, Frederick. "The Color Line." *The North American Review* 132 (1881): 567–577.

———. *Narrative of the Life of Frederick Douglass: An American Slave*. Edited by Benjamin Quarles. Cambridge, MA: Harvard University Press, 1988.

Dovidio John F. and Samuel L. Gaertner. "The Aversive Forms of Racism." In *Prejudice, Discrimination, and Racism*, edited by John F. Dovidio and Samuel L. Gaertner, 61–89. Orlando: Academic Press, 1986.

Du Bois, W. E. B. *An Appeal to the World: A Statement of Denial of Human Rights to Minorities in the Case of Citizens of Negro Descent in the United States of America and an Appeal to the United Nations for Redress*. New York: National Association for the Advancement of Colored People, 1947.

———. *The Autobiography of W. E. B. Du Bois: A Soliloquy on Viewing My Life from the Last Decade of its First Century*. New York: International Publishers, 1968.

———. *Black Reconstruction in America*. New York: Russell and Russell, 1963.

———. *Darkwater: Voices From Within the Veil*. New York: Harcourt, Brace, and Howe, 1920.

———. *Dusk of Dawn: Essay Towards an Autobiography of a Race*. New York: Harcourt Brace, 1940.

———. "The Negro and the Warsaw Ghetto." *Jewish Life* 6, no. 7 (1952): 14–15.

———. *The Philadelphia Negro: A Social Study*. New York: Schocken Books, 1967.

———. "Social Theory of W. E. B. Du Bois, The Negro and the Warsaw Ghetto." In Phil Zuckerman, *Jewish Life,* 45–6. Thousand Oaks: Pine Forge Press, 2004.

———. The Souls of Black Folk." *The Independent* 57 (1904): 2920.

———. *The Souls of Black Folk*. Edited by Henry Louis Gates Jr. and Terri Hume Oliver. New York and London: W. W. Norton and Company, 1999.

———. *The Suppression of the African Slave Trade in the United States of America, 1638–1870*. New York: The Social Science Press, 1954.

Fanon, Frantz. *Black Skins, White Masks*. London: MacGibbon and Kee, 1968.

Frazier, E. Franklin. *The Negro Church in America*. Liverpool: Liverpool University Press, 1964.

Gates Jr., Henry Louis. "The Souls of Black Folk at 100: Both Sides Now." *New York Times*, May 4, 2003. Accessed January 28, 2015. http://www.nytimes.com/2003/05/04/books/review/04GATEST.html.

Gilroy, Paul. *The Black Atlantic: Modernity and Double Consciousness*. London: Verso, 1993.

Hubbard, Dolan. *The Souls of Black Folk: 100 Years Later*. Columbia: University of Missouri Press, 2007.

Johnson, Greg. "W. E. B. Du Bois's The Philadelphia Negro." *Penn Current*, July 2, 2009. Accessed January 20, 2015. http://www.upenn.edu/pennnews/current/node/3997.

King Jr., Martin Luther. "Honoring Du Bois." The Centennial Address at Carnegie Hall in New York City, February 23, 1968.

Kipling, Rudyard. "The White Man's Burden." *McClure's Magazine* 12 (1899): 290–1.

Kousser, J. Morgan. *The Shaping of Southern Politics: Suffrage, Restriction and the Establishment of the One-Party South*, 1880–1910. New Haven: Yale University Press, 1974.

Lewis, David Levering. *W. E. B. Du Bois: Biography of a Race, 1868–1919*. New York: Henry Holt, 1993.

Lincoln, Eric. *Race, Religion and the Continuing American Dilemma*. New York: Hill and Wang, 1984.

Massey, Douglas and Nancy Denton. *American Apartheid: Segregation and the Making of the Underclass.* Cambridge, MA: Harvard University Press, 1993.

Obama, Barack. "Obama's NAACP Speech." The White House, Office of the Press Secretary. New York, July 16, 2009. Accessed January 28, 2015. http://www.whitehouse.gov/the-press-office/remarks-president-naacp-centennial-convention-07162009.

Sayad, Abdelmalek. *The Suffering of the Immigrant*. London: Polity, 2004.

Shaw, Albert. "The New Books: Notes on Recent American Publications." *American Monthly Review of Reviews* 28 (1903): 249.

Stovall, TaRessa. "Arts Festival Celebrates W. E. B. Du Bois and the Diaspora." *The Crisis* 110, no. 5 (2003): 48.

Wamba, Philippe. *Kinship: A Family's Journey in Africa and America*. New York: Dutton, 1999.

West, Cornel. "The Dilemma of the Black Intellectual." *Critical Quarterly* 29, no. 4 (1987): 39–52.

Wortham, Robert A. "Introduction to the Sociology of W. E. B. Du Bois." *Sociation Today* 3 (2005): 1.

Wright, Earl. "W. E. B. Du Bois and the Atlanta Sociological Laboratory." *Sociation Today* 3 (2005): 1.

Zamir, Shamoon. *Dark Voices: W. E. B. Du Bois and American Thought: 1888–1903*. Chicago: University of Chicago, 1995.

THE MACAT LIBRARY
BY DISCIPLINE

AFRICANA STUDIES

Chinua Achebe's *An Image of Africa: Racism in Conrad's Heart of Darkness*
W. E. B. Du Bois's *The Souls of Black Folk*
Zora Neale Huston's *Characteristics of Negro Expression*
Martin Luther King Jr's *Why We Can't Wait*
Toni Morrison's *Playing in the Dark: Whiteness in the American Literary Imagination*

ANTHROPOLOGY

Arjun Appadurai's *Modernity at Large: Cultural Dimensions of Globalisation*
Philippe Ariès's *Centuries of Childhood*
Franz Boas's *Race, Language and Culture*
Kim Chan & Renée Mauborgne's *Blue Ocean Strategy*
Jared Diamond's *Guns, Germs & Steel: the Fate of Human Societies*
Jared Diamond's *Collapse: How Societies Choose to Fail or Survive*
E. E. Evans-Pritchard's *Witchcraft, Oracles and Magic Among the Azande*
James Ferguson's *The Anti-Politics Machine*
Clifford Geertz's *The Interpretation of Cultures*
David Graeber's *Debt: the First 5000 Years*
Karen Ho's *Liquidated: An Ethnography of Wall Street*
Geert Hofstede's *Culture's Consequences: Comparing Values, Behaviors, Institutes and Organizations across Nations*
Claude Lévi-Strauss's *Structural Anthropology*
Jay Macleod's *Ain't No Makin' It: Aspirations and Attainment in a Low-Income Neighborhood*
Saba Mahmood's *The Politics of Piety: The Islamic Revival and the Feminist Subject*
Marcel Mauss's *The Gift*

BUSINESS

Jean Lave & Etienne Wenger's *Situated Learning*
Theodore Levitt's *Marketing Myopia*
Burton G. Malkiel's *A Random Walk Down Wall Street*
Douglas McGregor's *The Human Side of Enterprise*
Michael Porter's *Competitive Strategy: Creating and Sustaining Superior Performance*
John Kotter's *Leading Change*
C. K. Prahalad & Gary Hamel's *The Core Competence of the Corporation*

CRIMINOLOGY

Michelle Alexander's *The New Jim Crow: Mass Incarceration in the Age of Colorblindness*
Michael R. Gottfredson & Travis Hirschi's *A General Theory of Crime*
Richard Herrnstein & Charles A. Murray's *The Bell Curve: Intelligence and Class Structure in American Life*
Elizabeth Loftus's *Eyewitness Testimony*
Jay Macleod's *Ain't No Makin' It: Aspirations and Attainment in a Low-Income Neighborhood*
Philip Zimbardo's *The Lucifer Effect*

ECONOMICS

Janet Abu-Lughod's *Before European Hegemony*
Ha-Joon Chang's *Kicking Away the Ladder*
David Brion Davis's *The Problem of Slavery in the Age of Revolution*
Milton Friedman's *The Role of Monetary Policy*
Milton Friedman's *Capitalism and Freedom*
David Graeber's *Debt: the First 5000 Years*
Friedrich Hayek's *The Road to Serfdom*
Karen Ho's *Liquidated: An Ethnography of Wall Street*

John Maynard Keynes's *The General Theory of Employment, Interest and Money*
Charles P. Kindleberger's *Manias, Panics and Crashes*
Robert Lucas's *Why Doesn't Capital Flow from Rich to Poor Countries?*
Burton G. Malkiel's *A Random Walk Down Wall Street*
Thomas Robert Malthus's *An Essay on the Principle of Population*
Karl Marx's *Capital*
Thomas Piketty's *Capital in the Twenty-First Century*
Amartya Sen's *Development as Freedom*
Adam Smith's *The Wealth of Nations*
Nassim Nicholas Taleb's *The Black Swan: The Impact of the Highly Improbable*
Amos Tversky's & Daniel Kahneman's *Judgment under Uncertainty: Heuristics and Biases*
Mahbub Ul Haq's *Reflections on Human Development*
Max Weber's *The Protestant Ethic and the Spirit of Capitalism*

FEMINISM AND GENDER STUDIES

Judith Butler's *Gender Trouble*
Simone De Beauvoir's *The Second Sex*
Michel Foucault's *History of Sexuality*
Betty Friedan's *The Feminine Mystique*
Saba Mahmood's *The Politics of Piety: The Islamic Revival and the Feminist Subject*
Joan Wallach Scott's *Gender and the Politics of History*
Mary Wollstonecraft's *A Vindication of the Rights of Woman*
Virginia Woolf's *A Room of One's Own*

GEOGRAPHY

The Brundtland Report's *Our Common Future*
Rachel Carson's *Silent Spring*
Charles Darwin's *On the Origin of Species*
James Ferguson's *The Anti-Politics Machine*
Jane Jacobs's *The Death and Life of Great American Cities*
James Lovelock's *Gaia: A New Look at Life on Earth*
Amartya Sen's *Development as Freedom*
Mathis Wackernagel & William Rees's *Our Ecological Footprint*

HISTORY

Janet Abu-Lughod's *Before European Hegemony*
Benedict Anderson's *Imagined Communities*
Bernard Bailyn's *The Ideological Origins of the American Revolution*
Hanna Batatu's *The Old Social Classes And The Revolutionary Movements Of Iraq*
Christopher Browning's *Ordinary Men: Reserve Police Batallion 101 and the Final Solution in Poland*
Edmund Burke's *Reflections on the Revolution in France*
William Cronon's *Nature's Metropolis: Chicago And The Great West*
Alfred W. Crosby's *The Columbian Exchange*
Hamid Dabashi's *Iran: A People Interrupted*
David Brion Davis's *The Problem of Slavery in the Age of Revolution*
Nathalie Zemon Davis's *The Return of Martin Guerre*
Jared Diamond's *Guns, Germs & Steel: the Fate of Human Societies*
Frank Dikotter's *Mao's Great Famine*
John W Dower's *War Without Mercy: Race And Power In The Pacific War*
W. E. B. Du Bois's *The Souls of Black Folk*
Richard J. Evans's *In Defence of History*
Lucien Febvre's *The Problem of Unbelief in the 16th Century*
Sheila Fitzpatrick's *Everyday Stalinism*

Eric Foner's *Reconstruction: America's Unfinished Revolution, 1863-1877*
Michel Foucault's *Discipline and Punish*
Michel Foucault's *History of Sexuality*
Francis Fukuyama's *The End of History and the Last Man*
John Lewis Gaddis's *We Now Know: Rethinking Cold War History*
Ernest Gellner's *Nations and Nationalism*
Eugene Genovese's *Roll, Jordan, Roll: The World the Slaves Made*
Carlo Ginzburg's *The Night Battles*
Daniel Goldhagen's *Hitler's Willing Executioners*
Jack Goldstone's *Revolution and Rebellion in the Early Modern World*
Antonio Gramsci's *The Prison Notebooks*
Alexander Hamilton, John Jay & James Madison's *The Federalist Papers*
Christopher Hill's *The World Turned Upside Down*
Carole Hillenbrand's *The Crusades: Islamic Perspectives*
Thomas Hobbes's *Leviathan*
Eric Hobsbawm's *The Age Of Revolution*
John A. Hobson's *Imperialism: A Study*
Albert Hourani's *History of the Arab Peoples*
Samuel P. Huntington's *The Clash of Civilizations and the Remaking of World Order*
C. L. R. James's *The Black Jacobins*
Tony Judt's *Postwar: A History of Europe Since 1945*
Ernst Kantorowicz's *The King's Two Bodies: A Study in Medieval Political Theology*
Paul Kennedy's *The Rise and Fall of the Great Powers*
Ian Kershaw's *The "Hitler Myth": Image and Reality in the Third Reich*
John Maynard Keynes's *The General Theory of Employment, Interest and Money*
Charles P. Kindleberger's *Manias, Panics and Crashes*
Martin Luther King Jr's *Why We Can't Wait*
Henry Kissinger's *World Order: Reflections on the Character of Nations and the Course of History*
Thomas Kuhn's *The Structure of Scientific Revolutions*
Georges Lefebvre's *The Coming of the French Revolution*
John Locke's *Two Treatises of Government*
Niccolò Machiavelli's *The Prince*
Thomas Robert Malthus's *An Essay on the Principle of Population*
Mahmood Mamdani's *Citizen and Subject: Contemporary Africa And The Legacy Of Late Colonialism*
Karl Marx's *Capital*
Stanley Milgram's *Obedience to Authority*
John Stuart Mill's *On Liberty*
Thomas Paine's *Common Sense*
Thomas Paine's *Rights of Man*
Geoffrey Parker's *Global Crisis: War, Climate Change and Catastrophe in the Seventeenth Century*
Jonathan Riley-Smith's *The First Crusade and the Idea of Crusading*
Jean-Jacques Rousseau's *The Social Contract*
Joan Wallach Scott's *Gender and the Politics of History*
Theda Skocpol's *States and Social Revolutions*
Adam Smith's *The Wealth of Nations*
Timothy Snyder's *Bloodlands: Europe Between Hitler and Stalin*
Sun Tzu's *The Art of War*
Keith Thomas's *Religion and the Decline of Magic*
Thucydides's *The History of the Peloponnesian War*
Frederick Jackson Turner's *The Significance of the Frontier in American History*
Odd Arne Westad's *The Global Cold War: Third World Interventions And The Making Of Our Times*

The Macat Library By Discipline

LITERATURE

Chinua Achebe's *An Image of Africa: Racism in Conrad's Heart of Darkness*
Roland Barthes's *Mythologies*
Homi K. Bhabha's *The Location of Culture*
Judith Butler's *Gender Trouble*
Simone De Beauvoir's *The Second Sex*
Ferdinand De Saussure's *Course in General Linguistics*
T. S. Eliot's *The Sacred Wood: Essays on Poetry and Criticism*
Zora Neale Huston's *Characteristics of Negro Expression*
Toni Morrison's *Playing in the Dark: Whiteness in the American Literary Imagination*
Edward Said's *Orientalism*
Gayatri Chakravorty Spivak's *Can the Subaltern Speak?*
Mary Wollstonecraft's *A Vindication of the Rights of Women*
Virginia Woolf's *A Room of One's Own*

PHILOSOPHY

Elizabeth Anscombe's *Modern Moral Philosophy*
Hannah Arendt's *The Human Condition*
Aristotle's *Metaphysics*
Aristotle's *Nicomachean Ethics*
Edmund Gettier's *Is Justified True Belief Knowledge?*
Georg Wilhelm Friedrich Hegel's *Phenomenology of Spirit*
David Hume's *Dialogues Concerning Natural Religion*
David Hume's *The Enquiry for Human Understanding*
Immanuel Kant's *Religion within the Boundaries of Mere Reason*
Immanuel Kant's *Critique of Pure Reason*
Søren Kierkegaard's *The Sickness Unto Death*
Søren Kierkegaard's *Fear and Trembling*
C. S. Lewis's *The Abolition of Man*
Alasdair MacIntyre's *After Virtue*
Marcus Aurelius's *Meditations*
Friedrich Nietzsche's *On the Genealogy of Morality*
Friedrich Nietzsche's *Beyond Good and Evil*
Plato's *Republic*
Plato's *Symposium*
Jean-Jacques Rousseau's *The Social Contract*
Gilbert Ryle's *The Concept of Mind*
Baruch Spinoza's *Ethics*
Sun Tzu's *The Art of War*
Ludwig Wittgenstein's *Philosophical Investigations*

POLITICS

Benedict Anderson's *Imagined Communities*
Aristotle's *Politics*
Bernard Bailyn's *The Ideological Origins of the American Revolution*
Edmund Burke's *Reflections on the Revolution in France*
John C. Calhoun's *A Disquisition on Government*
Ha-Joon Chang's *Kicking Away the Ladder*
Hamid Dabashi's *Iran: A People Interrupted*
Hamid Dabashi's *Theology of Discontent: The Ideological Foundation of the Islamic Revolution in Iran*
Robert Dahl's *Democracy and its Critics*
Robert Dahl's *Who Governs?*
David Brion Davis's *The Problem of Slavery in the Age of Revolution*

Alexis De Tocqueville's *Democracy in America*
James Ferguson's *The Anti-Politics Machine*
Frank Dikotter's *Mao's Great Famine*
Sheila Fitzpatrick's *Everyday Stalinism*
Eric Foner's *Reconstruction: America's Unfinished Revolution, 1863-1877*
Milton Friedman's *Capitalism and Freedom*
Francis Fukuyama's *The End of History and the Last Man*
John Lewis Gaddis's *We Now Know: Rethinking Cold War History*
Ernest Gellner's *Nations and Nationalism*
David Graeber's *Debt: the First 5000 Years*
Antonio Gramsci's *The Prison Notebooks*
Alexander Hamilton, John Jay & James Madison's *The Federalist Papers*
Friedrich Hayek's *The Road to Serfdom*
Christopher Hill's *The World Turned Upside Down*
Thomas Hobbes's *Leviathan*
John A. Hobson's *Imperialism: A Study*
Samuel P. Huntington's *The Clash of Civilizations and the Remaking of World Order*
Tony Judt's *Postwar: A History of Europe Since 1945*
David C. Kang's *China Rising: Peace, Power and Order in East Asia*
Paul Kennedy's *The Rise and Fall of Great Powers*
Robert Keohane's *After Hegemony*
Martin Luther King Jr.'s *Why We Can't Wait*
Henry Kissinger's *World Order: Reflections on the Character of Nations and the Course of History*
John Locke's *Two Treatises of Government*
Niccolò Machiavelli's *The Prince*
Thomas Robert Malthus's *An Essay on the Principle of Population*
Mahmood Mamdani's *Citizen and Subject: Contemporary Africa And The Legacy Of Late Colonialism*
Karl Marx's *Capital*
John Stuart Mill's *On Liberty*
John Stuart Mill's *Utilitarianism*
Hans Morgenthau's *Politics Among Nations*
Thomas Paine's *Common Sense*
Thomas Paine's *Rights of Man*
Thomas Piketty's *Capital in the Twenty-First Century*
Robert D. Putman's *Bowling Alone*
John Rawls's *Theory of Justice*
Jean-Jacques Rousseau's *The Social Contract*
Theda Skocpol's *States and Social Revolutions*
Adam Smith's *The Wealth of Nations*
Sun Tzu's *The Art of War*
Henry David Thoreau's *Civil Disobedience*
Thucydides's *The History of the Peloponnesian War*
Kenneth Waltz's *Theory of International Politics*
Max Weber's *Politics as a Vocation*
Odd Arne Westad's *The Global Cold War: Third World Interventions And The Making Of Our Times*

POSTCOLONIAL STUDIES

Roland Barthes's *Mythologies*
Frantz Fanon's *Black Skin, White Masks*
Homi K. Bhabha's *The Location of Culture*
Gustavo Gutiérrez's *A Theology of Liberation*
Edward Said's *Orientalism*
Gayatri Chakravorty Spivak's *Can the Subaltern Speak?*

The Macat Library By Discipline

PSYCHOLOGY

Gordon Allport's *The Nature of Prejudice*
Alan Baddeley & Graham Hitch's *Aggression: A Social Learning Analysis*
Albert Bandura's *Aggression: A Social Learning Analysis*
Leon Festinger's *A Theory of Cognitive Dissonance*
Sigmund Freud's *The Interpretation of Dreams*
Betty Friedan's *The Feminine Mystique*
Michael R. Gottfredson & Travis Hirschi's *A General Theory of Crime*
Eric Hoffer's *The True Believer: Thoughts on the Nature of Mass Movements*
William James's *Principles of Psychology*
Elizabeth Loftus's *Eyewitness Testimony*
A. H. Maslow's *A Theory of Human Motivation*
Stanley Milgram's *Obedience to Authority*
Steven Pinker's *The Better Angels of Our Nature*
Oliver Sacks's *The Man Who Mistook His Wife For a Hat*
Richard Thaler & Cass Sunstein's *Nudge: Improving Decisions About Health, Wealth and Happiness*
Amos Tversky's *Judgment under Uncertainty: Heuristics and Biases*
Philip Zimbardo's *The Lucifer Effect*

SCIENCE

Rachel Carson's *Silent Spring*
William Cronon's *Nature's Metropolis: Chicago And The Great West*
Alfred W. Crosby's *The Columbian Exchange*
Charles Darwin's *On the Origin of Species*
Richard Dawkin's *The Selfish Gene*
Thomas Kuhn's *The Structure of Scientific Revolutions*
Geoffrey Parker's *Global Crisis: War, Climate Change and Catastrophe in the Seventeenth Century*
Mathis Wackernagel & William Rees's *Our Ecological Footprint*

SOCIOLOGY

Michelle Alexander's *The New Jim Crow: Mass Incarceration in the Age of Colorblindness*
Gordon Allport's *The Nature of Prejudice*
Albert Bandura's *Aggression: A Social Learning Analysis*
Hanna Batatu's *The Old Social Classes And The Revolutionary Movements Of Iraq*
Ha-Joon Chang's *Kicking Away the Ladder*
W. E. B. Du Bois's *The Souls of Black Folk*
Émile Durkheim's *On Suicide*
Frantz Fanon's *Black Skin, White Masks*
Frantz Fanon's *The Wretched of the Earth*
Eric Foner's *Reconstruction: America's Unfinished Revolution, 1863-1877*
Eugene Genovese's *Roll, Jordan, Roll: The World the Slaves Made*
Jack Goldstone's *Revolution and Rebellion in the Early Modern World*
Antonio Gramsci's *The Prison Notebooks*
Richard Herrnstein & Charles A Murray's *The Bell Curve: Intelligence and Class Structure in American Life*
Eric Hoffer's *The True Believer: Thoughts on the Nature of Mass Movements*
Jane Jacobs's *The Death and Life of Great American Cities*
Robert Lucas's *Why Doesn't Capital Flow from Rich to Poor Countries?*
Jay Macleod's *Ain't No Makin' It: Aspirations and Attainment in a Low Income Neighborhood*
Elaine May's *Homeward Bound: American Families in the Cold War Era*
Douglas McGregor's *The Human Side of Enterprise*
C. Wright Mills's *The Sociological Imagination*

Thomas Piketty's *Capital in the Twenty-First Century*
Robert D. Putman's *Bowling Alone*
David Riesman's *The Lonely Crowd: A Study of the Changing American Character*
Edward Said's *Orientalism*
Joan Wallach Scott's *Gender and the Politics of History*
Theda Skocpol's *States and Social Revolutions*
Max Weber's *The Protestant Ethic and the Spirit of Capitalism*

THEOLOGY

Augustine's *Confessions*
Benedict's *Rule of St Benedict*
Gustavo Gutiérrez's *A Theology of Liberation*
Carole Hillenbrand's *The Crusades: Islamic Perspectives*
David Hume's *Dialogues Concerning Natural Religion*
Immanuel Kant's *Religion within the Boundaries of Mere Reason*
Ernst Kantorowicz's *The King's Two Bodies: A Study in Medieval Political Theology*
Søren Kierkegaard's *The Sickness Unto Death*
C. S. Lewis's *The Abolition of Man*
Saba Mahmood's *The Politics of Piety: The Islamic Revival and the Feminist Subject*
Baruch Spinoza's *Ethics*
Keith Thomas's *Religion and the Decline of Magic*

COMING SOON

Chris Argyris's *The Individual and the Organisation*
Seyla Benhabib's *The Rights of Others*
Walter Benjamin's *The Work Of Art in the Age of Mechanical Reproduction*
John Berger's *Ways of Seeing*
Pierre Bourdieu's *Outline of a Theory of Practice*
Mary Douglas's *Purity and Danger*
Roland Dworkin's *Taking Rights Seriously*
James G. March's *Exploration and Exploitation in Organisational Learning*
Ikujiro Nonaka's *A Dynamic Theory of Organizational Knowledge Creation*
Griselda Pollock's *Vision and Difference*
Amartya Sen's *Inequality Re-Examined*
Susan Sontag's *On Photography*
Yasser Tabbaa's *The Transformation of Islamic Art*
Ludwig von Mises's *Theory of Money and Credit*

The Macat Library By Discipline

Printed in the United States
by Baker & Taylor Publisher Services